CONSEQUENCES OF LONGTERM CONFLICTS IN NORTHEAST INDIA

CONSEQUENCES OF LONGTERM CONFLICTS IN NORTHEAST INDIA

Editor

V.R. Raghavan

Published for

Centre for Security Analysis
Chennai, India

Vij Books India Pvt Ltd
New Delhi (India)

Published by

Vij Books India Pvt Ltd

2/19, Ansari Road, Darya Ganj
New Delhi - 110002
Phones: 91-11-65449971, 91-11- 43596460
Fax: 91-11-47340674
e-mail : vijbooks@rediffmail.com
web : www.vijbooks.com

Centre for Security Analysis
"9-B" Ninth Floor,
Chesney Nilgiri, 71, Ethiraj Salai,
Egmore, Chennai-600008
Tamil Nadu, India
+91-44-65291889
office@csa-chennai.org
www.csa-chennai.org

First Published : 2013

Paperback Edition 2015

Acknowledgement

The Centre for Security Analysis (CSA) has undertaken a three year research project **Internal Conflicts and Transnational Consequences** supported by the John D and Catherine T MacArthur Foundation. This volume is part of the ongoing project and its publication has been possible by the project grant.

The Editor places on record the assistance and support provided by Major General Arun Roye, Executive Director and Secretary, the Research Centre for Eastern and North Eastern Regional Studies (CENERS-K) Kolkata, in organizing the seminar on which this book is based.

Table of Contents

FOREWORD

Historians, strategic analysts and other scholars have been studying conflicts for quite some time focusing mostly on their causes. Internal conflicts which are endemic in South and Southeast Asia have existed since several decades. In most cases, the original causes of such conflicts have been subsumed by their lasting consequences. The long term consequences have been felt in all spheres of life – economy, governance, politics and the social fabric of the state, so much so that over a period of time these have become drivers of the conflict. Two or more generations who are born and grown in the conflict environment have eventually become major stakeholders of the conflict. In such situations, one cannot forever wait for total normalcy to return to undertake socio-political and economic development work. In the case of Northeast India, instability is characterized by two distinct factors – clashes between ethnic groups and political movements against the Central Government. The conflict dynamics range from insurgency for secession or for autonomy to problems of continuous inflow of migrants and fights over land and limited resources. Terrorism is the means through which this effort is operationalised. The democratic & governance deficits and the ways these problems have been addressed in fits and starts have added to the complexity of the conflicts.

The long term internal conflicts in India's Northeast and their consequences require attention of the central and state governments as well as think tanks and action oriented civil society organisations. There are both serious internal and external consequences which cannot be ignored and need equal attention. It is worth flagging the fact that Northeast India plays an important role in actualising India's *Look East Policy* of expanding its engagement with Southeast Asia.

Not being fully integrated with the rest of India, Northeastern region has languished economically as well as emotionally. Lack of transit facilities except through a narrow land corridor has added to the isolation of the region. Lack of investments because of geographical and political situation, internal strife and ethnic rivalry have been adding to the causes of non development. The Northeastern region borders more with neighbouring countries than mainland India and has the potential to play a major role as an economic and trade hub to realise the objectives of *Look East Policy.*

As part of its ongoing research project on internal conflicts in India, Myanmar, Nepal and Sri Lanka, the CSA organised a study in 2010 in collaboration with Centre for North-East Studies and Policy Research (C-NES). The papers generated through that study were presented at a seminar organised in New Delhi in July 2010, the proceedings of which stand published as an edited volume. The consequences of the conflict in Northeast India are so varied and vast, it was felt one such effort was not sufficient and it should be continued by associating more scholars and experts. Accordingly, another study was organised by engaging as many as eight scholars and experts to analyse many other dimensions of the consequences. These papers were presented at a seminar held in Kolkata on 26th October 2012, which was organised in collaboration with Research Centre for Eastern and North Eastern Regional Studies-Kolkata (CENERS-K). Both the studies put together provide a fuller view of the consequences covering political, economic, socio-ethnic and include impact of the countries surrounding the Northeast on India's foreign relations.

The CSA and CENERS-K are thankful to His Excellency Mr M K Narayanan, Governor of West Bengal for delivering an erudite keynote address which provided an enlightened backdrop and guidance for the subsequent presentations. Mr Narayanan remarked that the Northeast suffered from lack of transit facilities which aggravated the isolation; lack of investment had resulted in absence of development and special needs were often ignored or were not adequately appreciated. He also observed that many of the problems faced by the Northeast were similar to those faced by other parts of the nation and therefore the practice of "islanding" the problem of the Northeast should be resisted. Such an approach could turn out to be counterproductive and counter intuitive. The seminar should come out with solutions to the Northeast conflict which would be in sync with the prescription for other parts of India as well. It was heartening to note that subsequent speakers did appreciate the import of his observations and accordingly made their presentations. Mr Narayanan was a Founding Member of the Centre for Security Analysis and his joining the seminar was thus an additional pleasure and privilege.

The paper presenters have projected a realistic appreciation of the situation and have highlighted interesting and practical approaches to address the complex issues. This volume along with the earlier one provides wide ranging and significant insights into the dynamics of consequences of the conflict in Northeast region of India which will be useful for politicians, administrators and academic researchers.

V.R. Raghavan
President, Centre for Security Analysis

Keynote Address
Mr. M. K. Narayanan
Governor of West Bengal

I would like to thank the Centre for Security Analysis, Chennai and Research Centre for Eastern and Northeastern Regional Studies (CENERS-K), Kolkata for inviting me to inaugurate this Seminar on 'Long Term Consequences of Conflicts in North Eastern India'. The subject is hardly new. It has been discussed and debated at length, may be under different labels, for long. That the topic is still relevant only confirms that the problem is one that continues to defy solution. This is often the case with many of our long-standing problems.

The concept note for the Seminar set me thinking. The analysis of the situation prevailing in the Northeast makes it appear that the situation has changed little, despite the passage of time. Consequently, the prescriptions and remedies expected are likely to be similar to those prescribed earlier.

I, for one, do not think that time has stood still in the Northeast. There are many more, and newer, issues that exist in the Northeast today. There are commonalities between what is happening there and in the rest of the country, especially when it comes to the security aspects. I hold the view that the practice of 'islanding' the problems of the Northeast, and treating these as totally different from those of the rest of India, could turn out to be counterproductive and counterintuitive.

I, hence, wondered whether this Seminar would be willing to be a Seminar with a difference. Would the participants be willing to look at problems of the Northeast from a different standpoint?

In my preambular remarks, I am willing to go along with some of the common perceptions of the problems that afflict the Northeast and its people, which also find a mention in the concept note. However, I would urge that the distance between the NE and the rest of India on these counts should not be exaggerated.

It is true that persons from the Northeast feel strongly that they lack acceptance outside their normal habitat. Many Northeasterners nurse concerns about their personal safety when they travel to different corners of the country – the recent mass exodus of North Easterners from cities like Bangalore, Hyderabad, Pune, etc., based on mischievous e-messages, was an instance, though an extreme one, of this kind. On a lesser magnitude, perhaps, I dare say that even people from the South or Bihar today nurse similar fears about their safety even in a cosmopolitan city like Mumbai. People from the Northeast also complain that they suffer many indignities when they travel in India. Unfortunately, it is a fact that as a nation we tend to look down upon people who look different, speak a different language and follow different customs.

Admittedly, the Northeast does suffer from lack of transit facilities which aggravate feelings of isolation. Lack of investment has resulted in an absence of development. Special needs of the region are often ignored, or not adequately appreciated, but often enough such complaints can be heard from other parts of the country as well. On one parameter, viz., that of obligation to social harmony, the Northeast can possibly claim to be better off than the rest of India, where indifference to such obligations has become the norm.

Coming to basic causes of conflict in the Northeast, if I were to reduce these to a set of issues and principles, then perhaps the gap between the situation in the Northeast and that prevailing in the rest of India may not seem so vast. Governance issues, or more appropriately, lack of governance, fragmentation of political power, and an excessive region-centric calculus afflict not only the States of the Northeast, but almost every State in the country. While the Northeast has for long suffered due to lack of internal cohesion, this syndrome now affects most, if not all, states of the country. Internal strife and ethnic/caste rivalry which has kept the Northeast from realizing its full potential is now endemic to most parts of the country, adversely affecting their progress.

What I am driving at is that it is no longer proper to view events in the Northeast as if they are totally removed from developments in other parts of our country. The fact is that there are extensive linkages today between conflicts in the Northeast and those in the rest of the country today. It is important to recognize this.

We should instead acknowledge that we are meeting at a time when the country as a whole, and not only the Northeast, is facing complex challenges. There is today a strengthening of fissiparous and centrifugal tendencies across the nation. These tendencies are no longer confined to the Northeast. The long term consequences for the nation are as grave, unless we can sustain a strong sense of nationhood. We need to respond to such challenges in a holistic manner.

When we come to the security calculus in the Northeast, which is an important subtext of the topic under discussion, again there has to be a realization that the security matrix here is made up of many imponderable factors, several of which exist outside the region. Any kind of compartmentalization would be ill-advised.

For example, what I would like to point out is that what we are witnessing across the nation today, is a concerted assault on our composite culture. This is not limited only to the Northeast. Ethnic and religious communities that have lived side by side with each other are now in open conflict. Fault lines are becoming wider, and clashes more intense and violent. There are forces at work which are deliberately encouraging an atmosphere of hatred and violence. Militant outfits are proliferating in many places. The Northeast is, hence, hardly an example.

Some of this may have to do with prevailing trends in the 21st century that we see across the globe. Terrorism has today mutated into a global franchise. Ideology based movements are gaining in strength. Cyber warfare, which though still evolving, has already become a hydra-headed monster.

Perhaps more serious, is the growth of fundamentalist and extremist ideas. These are spreading at a speed that is frightening. Religious fundamentalism is becoming more threatening and events of recent weeks, and the rage and violence that followed the airing of the documentary *Innocence of Muslims*, cannot be solely attributed to spontaneity. 'Organized rage' seems no longer confined to fringe groups, but are becoming part of the mainstream.

Coming to the long term consequences of the conflicts taking place in the Northeast, it is not my intention to minimize the differences that exist between what exists there and that prevailing in the rest of India. The strategic location of the Northeast, years of semi-insurgency fuelled in substantial measure by external forces, perceived distance from mainland India, and geopolitical interests of regional players certainly make the situation here more complex and challenging.

There are also other factors present today. Ethnic sub-nationalism and identity politics have an additional dimension where the Northeast is concerned. Here ethnic allegiance is oftentimes in conflict with mainstream nationalism or vice versa. This manifests itself in different ways, but the subliminal message is that often enough in the Northeast, primordial and ethnic identities overwhelm all other considerations.

Additionally, issues of autonomy and immigration have again gained a great deal of traction here lately. The 'outsider-insider' syndrome is reemerging in a more virulent form. More than anything else, a whole new panorama of sub-state actors – operating as near-State entities – has emerged. Many have embedded themselves within the political system seriously impacting stability in the region.

Dealing with the narrative of fundamentalism in the region will prove to be one of the most challenging tasks for authorities in the region. All this is creating an impression that there are too many disparate forces pulling in different directions, as far as the Northeast is concerned.

Assam, which was perceived as, possibly, the most stable of the 'Seven Sisters of the North East', has become a new cauldron of conflict. The euphoria that was seen when the United Liberation Front of Assam split into a majority Pro-talk and minority Anti-talk faction has ebbed. ULFA inspired militancy is on the rise, targeting Security Forces and non-Assamese.

Likewise, the splintering of many militant factions, as for instance, the DHD-J in Karbe Anglong and NC Hills, has not brought the hoped for peace. Not only have splintered factions tended to be more aggressive, but several 'copycat' outfits have sprung up, hoping to occupy the space temporarily vacated by the major players. Consequently, the conventional view that ethnic uprisings are an expression of the aspirations of the marginalized wanting to find a voice in the political discourse of the day, is clearly off the mark.

There are a number of simultaneous fires raging in Assam at present. An impression is sought to be created that its political resources are inadequate to tackle these simultaneous threats. While the recent ethnic clashes between tribals, mainly Bodos, and others, mainly Muslims, in the territory of the Bodoland Territorial Areas District, was unprecedented in terms of the violence and the displacement of population, it essentially highlighted the underlying tensions present in the State. Recent reports of consolidation efforts by other tribals like Adivasis, as also the Minorities, further confirm the existence of such tensions. New Adivasi and Muslim militant groups are springing up as a result.

Many issues which were treated as settled, have been reopened, particularly the vexed issue of infiltration of Bangladeshi Muslims into the Northeast. The concerns expressed by Bodo groups in the BTAD, viz., that of changing demographics and consequential land alienation, are now being echoed across Assam and some of the other NE States.

The issue is unlikely to die down in the near future, since it has become a rallying cry across the region. Large numbers of Muslims are now being viewed with suspicion as 'illegal immigrants' and are at the receiving end of the ire of the rest of the population. Strengthening of Muslim fundamentalist organizations in the State over time has complicated matter.

In both Manipur and Nagaland, we see a resurgence of ultra-nationalist tendencies. In Manipur, an open confrontation can be seen between Meitei nationalism and Naga ultra-radicalism, especially in the Hill districts of the State. Meitei underground outfits such as the RPF/PLA and the UNLF have been successful in whipping Meitei chauvinism, and in consolidating their position in the State and across the region. They have acquired a significant profile through their strategy of networking with other Northeast insurgent outfits.

The PLA is today an important link also between the Northeast militants and Maoists in the hinterland States of the country. A clandestine nexus with Chinese arms suppliers in Kunming in China is also being attempted.

In Nagaland, ultra radical Naga nationalism is gaining ascendency at the expense of so-called moderates. New para-insurgent outfits are coming up, the intention being to carry out recruitment from the so-called Nagalim areas of Nagaland, Manipur, Assam and Arunachal Pradesh. The Peoples' Democratic Volunteer Force is being projected as the first line of defence against any offensive by Security Forces against the Nagas. Creation of such a pan-Naga outfit is a dangerous trend and will have serious consequences for the region.

There are few areas in the Northeast that do not face problems of one kind or the other. Tripura has been relatively quiet, but attempts at revival of insurgency led by the National Liberation Front of Tripura (BD) can be seen today. The NLFT (BD) seeks to be part of the wider insurgency patterns of the NE. In Meghalaya, groups like the HNLC – a Khasi militant outfit, and the Garo National Liberation Army – a Garo outfit – are both engaged in localized violence, seeking fulfillment of their demands.

In Arunachal Pradesh, local tribals have been quiescent so far, but the two main Naga factions, from Nagaland, viz., the NSCN (IM) and the NSCN (K), are engaged in a battle for supremacy in the Naga inhabited districts of Tirap and Changlang. China has not intruded into any of these calculations, as of now.

I have attempted to bring a different perspective to bear to the situation prevailing in the Northeast. I have done so by highlighting the many commonalities rather than the differences that exist presently between the situation in the Northeast and that in the rest of India.

It is critically important to arrive at a proper assessment of the situation, and also ensure proper comprehension of the factors, as well as forces, at work in the region. This would enable better understanding of the situation, viz. that it is not very dissimilar to what is happening in the rest of India.

I am hence of the view that it would be a mistake to try and find standalone solutions to the problems affecting the Northeast today. What exists in the Northeast of India is a microcosm of what exists in many other regions of the country. We must not treat the Northeast as a distinct, separate and different entity. The solutions that we seek should be compatible with those that apply to the rest of India. These could, perhaps, be tweaked to some extent to deal with the diversities of the Northeast region. I rest my case with this assertion.

Overview

K Srinivasan and Ancy Joseph

The Centre for Security Analysis (CSA), as part of its project to study the internal conflicts and their consequences has been engaging a number of researchers, social scientists and academics to analyse the causes and consequences of conflicts in India, Myanmar, Nepal and Sri Lanka. These studies have been presented at seminars held at various places in India, Singapore, Colombo and Kathmandu.

Conflict in Northeastern part of India in some ways is akin to other conflicts and it also differs in many other ways. The ethnic identity politics and inter-group rivalries and consequences thereof are more visible in the Northeast. The need to preserve the unique identity, culture, linguistics and customs of the Northeastern people was always recognised and respected. The Central Government has been consciously working to address the causes and consequences over the years. It has employed force to bring down the level of insurgency to create conditions for peaceful settlement of conflicts while simultaneously engaging in peace negotiations, empowering ethnic majorities and also working towards development with liberal economic packages. The approach has been not to assimilate the different ethnic identities but to accommodate them as part of nation building. In the process, seven states have been created. There is a criticism to say that such an effort has added to the problem. It has been seen that the conflict still persists between ethnic majority and minorities within Northeastern states and also between different tribal groups within the majority ethnic groups. The conflicts within inter and intra ethnic groups have risen over the years to gain political & economic power, land and uninterrupted practice of individual tribal tradition. The consequences of such conflicts have also resulted in law and order problem, corruption, rent collection, arms & drug smuggling and other underground activities. Internal displacements, immigration from neighbouring Bangladesh have added to the problem.

Changing demographics and internecine warfare have added new dimensions to the ongoing conflicts in the Northeast. Physical isolation of the Northeastern region is unique to this conflict. The feeling of neglect, a sense of deprivation and lack of respect for their unique identity have also been expressed in many fora. Lack of development and employment opportunities and lack of investment has been highlighted by many others. This aspect has been stated to be a cause as well as a consequence of the conflict. In order to study these issues, the CSA organized two studies to address the different dimensions of the conflict. One such set of studies were presented at a conference in New Delhi in 2010 and the same stands published as an edited volume.

Conflict in Northeast has many dimensions and its consequences are many layered. Northeast India is home to over 200 different ethnic groups and subgroups and over 400 linguistic groups, many of whom have distinct political interests and claims and are in conflict both with each other and with the Central and state governments. Conflicts prevail in four of the seven states - Assam, Nagaland, Manipur and Mizoram. These insurgencies range from secession to autonomy, movement against outsiders and immigrants and ethnic differences. The Naga tribe of the region has a demand of greater Nagaland. They want geographical expansion of the Nagaland into its adjacent state of Manipur where the Naga has been traditionally living. In order to achieve this goal, National Socialist Council of Nagaland (NSCN) has been formed. Similarly, various militant outfits in Assam are embroiled in armed conflicts against the state and also against people illegally migrated from Bangladesh. Insurgent groups like the United Liberation Front of Assam (ULFA), Bodo People's Action Committee (BPAC), Bodo Security Force (BSF), Bodo Liberation Tiger Force (BLTF), and National Democratic Front for Bodoland (NDFB) are the main outfits of the region which have badly affected the lives of the people. Similarly the People's Liberation Army (PLA) and United National Liberation Front (UNLF) of Manipur and the All Tripura Tribal Force (ATTP) are embroiled in armed conflicts against the lawfully established governments in the respective states. The democratic and governance deficits and the manner these problems have been addressed in fits and starts have added to the complexity of the conflicts.

Northeast India plays an important role in actualising India's Look East Policy. Not fully integrated with the rest of India, Northeastern region has languished economically as well as emotionally. Lack of transit facilities except through a narrow corridor has added to the isolation of the region. Lack of investments because of geographical condition, internal strife and ethnic rivalry have been adding to the causes of non development. Northeastern region borders more with neighbouring countries than mainland India and has the potential to play a major role of economic and trade hub to realise the objectives of *Look East Policy*. While it is generally agreed that such conflicts have serious internal consequences, they also have external consequences which cannot be ignored and need equal attention.

CSA in collaboration with Research Centre for Eastern and Northeastern Regional Studies (CENERS-K), Kolkata organized a seminar "Long Term Consequences of Conflicts in North Eastern India" at Kolkata in October 2012. The Seminar provided a platform for researchers and strategic thinkers to examine and explore the different dimensions of these conflicts in Northeast India and find practical and worthwhile solutions. Eight research papers covering various facets of the conflicts were presented at the Seminar. Mr M K Narayanan, Governor of West Bengal delivered the Keynote Address.

Falguni Rajkumar traces the causes of the ethnic divide to the policies adopted by the colonial rulers, who introduced restrictions of movement by the inner line and also by bringing in Christianity to the uplands. Post independence, this was further aggravated by segregating them as scheduled tribes. He maintains that the decades long insurgency in the Northeast has accentuated the ethnic identity politics in the region. This in turn has affected the social–cultural dimension of inter–ethnic relationship, law and order and has hindered the peacemaking efforts. He argues that the adverse fallout of these acrimonious polities in the region and assertive ethnic identity have greatly impacted development and economy of the region. As a recommendation to overcome these challenges, he suggests a shift in emphasis to address the economic and development needs of people in the region will not only wean away people from their preoccupation with their ethnic identities, coupled with governmental efforts to down play the security oriented approach in solving the problems of the region, a much more conducive environment will be created, wherein peace stands a better chance to survive. In today's globalized world, the states in the Northeastern region cannot exist in 'isolation' as they had done in the past by trying to define themselves as separate small silos of exclusivity. They need to instead find ways and means to come closer together for economic prosperity and shifting their priorities from their preoccupation with divisive identity politics to one of cooperation and partnership among themselves. From this perspective, there is an urgent need to overcome the unfortunate prevailing atmosphere of mistrust and acrimonious equations among the people and states in the region. As to the employment of Army to rein in law and order, he refers to an observation made by a former Judge Advocate General (JAG) of the Indian Army, Major General Nilendra Kumar (Retd) that there is a need to educate and connect the personnel of the security forces to the tribal cultural environment and various subtle nuances of the socio-political aspects of the people amidst whom they are expected to operate. The NER needs a peace process that addresses these issues holistically. Peace efforts have to be comprehensive, regional in content and in context emphasizing on its role as means to bridge the ethnic divide. It must create a set of unique values, capable of addressing and assuaging the psychological anxieties and fears of all concerned. To achieve this government needs to choose a different path quite distinct from what has already been tried in the past. He further argues that if the government and the people of the region shift the focus of human relationships to the notion of 'belongingness', the 'softer' side of peoples' experiences and associations, an alternative way to deal with the problem of ethnic relationships may perhaps be found.

Monalisa Changkija in her paper analyses the conflict dynamics in Nagaland and points out that besides the usual conflicts that insurgency and militancy pose to any society in any part of the globe, perhaps often forgotten and ignored are the conflicts entrenched in tribalism, conflicting aspirations and interests, cultural diversities and dreams and schemes of tribal hegemony, as also power struggles at various levels of society due to multiplicity of value systems. These conflicts are harder to deal with, especially through and with modern concepts such as democracy and institutions which are alien to these primordial societies. She explains the issues with a case study of a tribal village in Nagaland. She underscores the fact that standing at the crossroads of the tradition and modernity, people of Nagaland are not very sure as to how to view and what to make out of the rapidly-changing equations that they see locally, regionally, nationally and globally. This has disoriented them and this disorientation has spawned conflicts that have hitherto been ignored, neglected or simply brushed off as extraneous to the larger scheme of things of matters Northeast. She highlights that multiplicity of systems of governance, both constitutional and traditional that not only have confused the Naga mind but also have created the space and scope for more conflicts, which all go towards aggravating a tensed situation further leading to alienation and marginalization of the individual Naga from being a productive member of society and state. She critically looks at the Look East Policy and its implications on Nagaland. She argues that unless the Look East Policy is unambiguously spelled out as it affects the lives of people in the Northeast there is much scope for social upheavals in this region. According to her, the infrastructure required to implement Look East Policy would environmentally and otherwise affect the Nagas. She recommends scrapping of AFSPA and setting up of a Ministry for Human Security Development to be manned by expert from various fields.

Samir Kar Purukayastha in his paper looks extensively at the conflict situations in states of Assam, Mizoram, Meghalaya and Tripura. According to Samir, there has been a reduction in militancy in Assam. This is attributed to drooping morale and diminishing cadre strength of various insurgent groups, loss of safe havens across the borders viz, Bhutan, Bangladesh and Myanmar. Moreover, the people are no longer sympathetic to these rebels as they started targeting innocent civilians. Though Mizo Accord is considered to be the most successful peace accord signed in the Northeastern region, Hmar insurgency and issues of Bru refugees have dented the peace in Mizoram. Ethnic identity politics have pushed Meghalaya into a state of crisis. Tripura has successfully contained insurgency through well planned counter-insurgency operations coupled with governance and development interventions. He assesses that a broad picture that is emerging today in Northeast is in favour of peace. The people are pressurizing the militant groups for peace negotiations. But this however does not indicate end of insurgency. Unfortunately, being a highly heterogeneous region, concessions and compromises granted to reconcile a specific group often alienates another. He recommends that the process of conflict resolution should not heavily rely on the talks-bound militant leaders, who are often pushy, unreasonable and unaccommodating. Rather, attempt should be made to win over the support of the common people, who only want a decent earning and lead a dignified life.

Jayanta Kumar Ray in his paper examines the recent ethnic clashes in Bodoland, which is seen as an offshoot of the old conflict between the tribals and non- tribals. He refers to the illegal migration of Bangladeshi Muslims and asserts that the Bangladeshi Muslim migrants have set up militant groups to carve out a separate Muslin state in Bodoland and maintains that the issue of infiltration from Bangladesh should not be downplayed. He critizes that New Delhi and Guwahati have failed to plan appropriate measures to cope with these illegal migrations as the political circles view them as a vote bank. He recommends identification of illegal immigrants and their deportation in large numbers.

Arun Roye, to begin with explores the political developments within Myanmar and the problems therein. He has highlighted the geographic importance of Myanmar vis-à-vis India, China and Southeast Asian countries. He has identified major ethnic groups on the periphery of Myanmar as well as the ethnic problems between the Government and ethnic armies. He also highlights the collaborative activities of Indian insurgent groups operating in Northeast India with those of Myanmar. He has analysed the impact of these activities on India – Myanmar relations and he has suggested a few steps to improve the situation.

P D Rai in his paper examines the impact of conflicts in Northeast on Nepal and Bhutan and its offset on Sikkim. He recommends trade with China through Nathu La Pass be expanded as we have done with Pakistan at Wagha Border. Eco tourism to Northeast is another area to be exploited. Then he also points out that soft power, through the people of 'Nepali ethnicity' may be used as a cultural and people's bridge to bolster the diplomatic efforts to 'wean' Nepal away from the Chinese cultural and economic influences. Central to this will be the address of the growing 'trust deficit'. A long term program can be formulated at the earliest. In Bhutan, efforts need to continue to help them become a more vibrant democracy.

Thapliyal in his paper gives an overview of the Conflicts in Northeast India and explores the responses of Central government to curb these conflicts. The only insurgency that has been successfully resolved has been that of Mizoram. In absence of effective governing structures in the states, the financial assistance doled out by the Centre often finds its way to the insurgent groups. This indirectly perpetuates the insurgency in these states. He is critical of the general ideas being discussed about economic development of the Northeastern region. He opines that the propagation of new variant of the "development solution" is facile lacking in connect with the realities of the ground. It is a pure theoretical macroeconomic orientation with a deliberate neglect of the peculiarities of the political economy of the region. He points out that market integration across the borders will result in many problems under the present circumstances. The state of governance within Northeastern states and international relations with the countries in the region are to be taken into account before looking at a macroeconomic scene and full implementation of the Look East Policy through this region. He observes that India's relations with neighbouring countries are riddled with political and diplomatic minefields. Bangladesh has had a long history of overt and covert hostility. Border disputes and the memory of 1962 place China in the realm of perpetual suspicion. While India's relations with Myanmar are friendly, but China's overwhelming presence in Myanmar will, again, create potential difficulties and areas of suspicion. China's aggressive expansion across South East Asia and in the Indian neighbourhood is also perceived as a significant threat – both in economic and security terms. Given existing political relationships in the neighbourhood, the actual realization of trade potential is constrained. He accepts that military solutions alone cannot curb insurgency; political consolidation must follow success achieved by conduct of military operations against the insurgents. It thus emerges that politico – military synergy is the sine qua non for a solution. He goes to list a number of aspects wherein such synergy is required. He recommends setting up of an expert group by the Centre to evolve policy, monitor and where required order execution of plans and policy, so as to achieve conflict resolution. He stresses on total synergy amongst various intelligence agencies, setting up a Psychological Operations cell by the state governments in concert with the local Army formations and politico-military cooperation in far flung areas to ensure smooth execution and monitor progress of developmental projects and evolving an institutionalized system of taking inputs from the Army as well. He also looks at the merits and demerits of AFSPA, role of illegal migrants and external linkages of the insurgent groups in Northeast region. He asserts that to achieve conflict resolution, political consensus across party lines is essential, so as to formulate an implementable and cogent strategy.

Gulshan Sachdeva in his paper "Economic Consequences of Conflicts in Northeast India" analyses the policies of Central government for the regional development under various Five Year Plans. He points out that the policy framework for the region was guided by combination of political economy and culture. The main focus of political economy approach was on the relation between state and the economy with emphasis on the role of bureaucratic apparatus. The cultural approach focused on the socially constructed character of economic organisation wherein the economic system is the product of social order. He further argues that failure of economic strategy for the region is not because of any so-called economic neglect but because of wrong assumptions and inappropriate economic policy framework, which have created an unbalanced economy and destroyed the basic institutions of market economy. The states in this region have underdeveloped agrarian societies, with weak industrial sector mainly developed around tea, oil, timber and mining and inflated service sectors. He writes that there is an urgent need to question usual myths surrounding the region. He further writes that Centre's policy of protective discrimination have created more problems. He also negates the neglect theory and asserts that the lack of development is not because of the shortage of funds, in fact a large portion of the funds ends in the hands of insurgent groups. Despite the issues of illegal migration, major parts of the region face labour shortages and this is one of the main reasons for the failure of various labour intensive government schemes. He also examines the Look East Policy, the need to create market institutions and linking the region with the ASEAN neighbours. To take full advantage from its proximity to the ASEAN market, the region needs some fundamental changes in its land and labour policies in addition to improvements in infrastructure and security situation in some of the states. In the absence of these factors, the region will continue to depend on public investments for growth and development.

Consequences of long-Term Conflicts in North Eastern States

Falguni Rajkumar

Introduction

The long-term conflict in the Northeastern Region of India (NER) masquerading as ethno-nationalistic aspirations is assertive ethnic identity politics. There are several factors that have gone into transforming and making the peace loving and egalitarian people of the NER into a set of intolerant people preoccupied with their respective ethnic identities. The dramatic transformation is also largely due to the preoccupation of the Government with security of the region overlooking and neglecting the region's developmental needs in post-independent India.

The paper is divided into three main Sections. In part one of Section I the paper takes a brief overview of the various factors responsible for rise of ethnic identity politics, the main cause of insurgency and how this has over the years, due to its persistence, adversely affected the lives of people in the region. The second part, the inability of the government as well as the security forces involved to foresee the deleterious ability of the ethnic identity problem as the major source influencing and perpetuating the insurgency movements are discussed. And in the third part, the adverse impact or fall-out of these factors on the ongoing peace process and on the various peace accords already in place is dealt.

Section II of the paper suggests various possible ways to overcome the problems in these three identified areas.

Section III, examines the prevailing views and perceptions of people in the country about the NER, and how the ill informed views and opinions have over the years adversely affected the morale of the people of the NER and also of the country as a whole. This Section also touches upon the need of why it is important for all concerned to project appropriately and diligently the much improved prevailing law and order situation in the NER across the country so that the national prejudice about the people and the region can be corrected if not totally removed.

Section I

Insurgency in the Northeast: Who is to blame:

Understanding the various factors responsible for insurgency in the Northeastern region (NER) will provide the necessary backdrop in appreciating the consequences of the long-term conflicts that has inflicted on the people of the NER in particular and the country in general.

There are several influences and causes which are responsible for the rise of insurgency and ethnic identity politics in the NER. From historical perspective, these influences were introduced by the British in pre-independent India and the Government of India (GOI) after independence. Both these influences were exogenous factors that were beyond the control of the people of the NER. In addition, the trend of the British government as well as GOI to deal with the NER primarily from the security perspective because of its strategic location and the GOI by overlooking the economic development of the region were major factors that were largely responsible for the rise of assertive ethnic identity politics. In short, insurgency, militancy and the consequential ethnic identity problems are by products of the circumstances of the region's troubled political history.

The initial steps were taken by the British-India Government mischievously and insensitively by differentiating people between those living in the uplands and higher recesses from those living in the lowlands of the NER deliberately as part of the British frontier policy to control and govern the strategically important and politically sensitive frontier province of its empire. This 'divide' is responsible for arousing the sub-conscious racial and ethnic differences among the various ethnic groups. The 'Bengal Eastern Frontier Regulation' of 1873 formally introduced the 'inner line' permit system prohibiting the entry of all people into the highland areas occupied by the upland tribal communities. The administrative delineation of areas known as 'Excluded Areas' and 'Partially Excluded Areas' that followed in 1935 gave a new format of administering the areas occupied by the upland communities of the region. The 'Coupland Plan', the 'Crown

Colony' and other ideas and formulations were all intended to segregate and divide the people of the NER based on ethnic and socio-cultural differences. All these policies were intended to keep the two sets of people apart and divided so that they did not combine to fight the British.

In addition, the British administration gave permission to the Christian missionaries to convert the upland communities even though they advocated the preservation of the socio-cultural identity distinctivity of the upland people and communities. This decision to introduce Christianity further divided the people on religious lines between the lowland Hindus and the Christianised upland people. The 'divide' has geopolitically and socio-culturally polarized the entire region completely thereafter.

Even though the concept and idea of ethnic identity distinctivity was introduced in the region by the British, it is also the subsequent policies of the government in post-independent India, especially its inability to understand the complex nature and dynamics of the ethnic identity related issues and the nuances involved, which have all combined to compound the problem of the region. For instance, the distinction between upland tribal communities and the lowland non-tribal population prior to the distinctions made by the British, merely meant two sets of people living two distinct sets of life-styles in two separate and different geographical areas of the region. It neither had the socio-religious baggage nor the connotation of the backward tag descriptively or contextually that is attached today in the country by categorising the upland tribal group as 'Scheduled Tribe' under the Constitution of India.

Today, because of the constitutionally enforced 'distinction' a legal 'division' has been introduced between those who are categorised and defined as 'Scheduled Tribes' and those who are not. Such categorisations in a region like the NER where scores if not hundreds of ethnic groups are squeezed in a small geographical area in one of the remotest corners of the country has led to the complete polarization of people creating social tensions and chaos by dividing people and communities on ethnic lines. This unfortunate development is tragic because in a way it is a complete negation and countermanding of the socio-cultural links, ties and bonds that once characterised and defined people to people relationships in the NER. Its beginning marked the end of ethno-socio and cultural pluralism and camaraderie the region was well known for.

Nature & Impact of Conflict

Insurgency and its related conflicts in the NER had geopolitically taken two forms. (a) The conflict between the nation-state and one or more of its constituent member ethnic groups, which directly challenges and threatens the unity and sovereignty of the country and the nation. And (b), the conflicts and clashes between two or more constituent members of ethnic groups, which normally falls in the category of internal law and order problems and do not necessarily or directly threaten the unity or question the sovereignty of the country. However, over the years due to prolonged insurgency this too has morphed into open ethnic animosity and often ends in ethnic clashes. In a way, the phenomenon has militarised the communities and societies of the region. It has consequently driven the politics of assertive ethnic identity (ethno-nationalistic aspirations) from the jungles into drawing rooms and from there to the streets of the region, and in a way from the realms of the academia to reality.

Ethnic identity politics in the NER has adversely affected three key areas. These are

(i)   The socio-cultural dimension affecting ethnic relationships, which adversely affects inter-state (states within India) relations and in turn retards economic partnership for development of the region as a whole.

(ii) It adversely affects the maintenance of law and order in the region.

(iii) Causes a major obstacle to the on-going peace efforts between the government and the insurgent groups. These three aspects are discussed below.

Ethnic Identity Divide:Socio-Cultural Dimension

The most glaring direct adverse impact and consequence of the prolonged insurgency movements on the NER is the emergence of divisive ethnic identity politics affecting the general life and conditions in the region cutting across the ethnic divide without any exception. It has introduced the politics of rivalry and intolerance in a region once known for its egalitarian and composite culture. In fact, the social consequences of ethnic identity related violence and belligerence impact the people and the region psychologically within, and this in a way has adversely affected the polity of the region in the long run much more profoundly. This is simply because the psychological polarized ethnic divide has introduced its own politics of divide based on ethnic distinctivity than it did ever before. It has ingrained a ruthless sensibility among the post-independent generations of Northeast Indians who today look and deal with their neighbours in the region more as adversaries rather than as friends, a distinct departure from what their forefathers once did. The politics of the region is now highly volatile, coloured and overshadowed as it does with doubt and suspicions among people in the region about each other.

This in turn has affected as region geo-politically. Interstate and intrastate relations have never been so bad politically since the states, which were formed on ethnic lines. Today states act and deal with each other more as adversaries rather than as partners in jointly trying to overcome the various difficulties and constraints imposed by the physical features of the region for economic development. The polity is as such highly divided ethnically, highly partisan in character, which is exploited by political entrepreneurs adversely affecting not only relationships among people but also affecting and impacting governance and administration.

The adverse fallout of the acrimonious polity in the region has greatly impacted development and economy of the region; the NER (the erstwhile state of Assam), which at the time of independence was among the top few states in the country in terms of economic development, today finds itself at the bottom of the ladder. The region is underdeveloped and its performances being far below the national averages and is considered highly disjointed. In one way, the NER today comprises of many politically desirable states formed on expedient ethnic identity considerations but which are sadly economically and financially non-viable entities incapable of standing on their own revenues without financial support and assistance for their sustenance from the Central government.

Law and Order

In initiating this part of the paper, one is compelled to quote Sun Tzu from his famous treatise 'Art of War', who observed *"Subjugating the enemy's army without fighting is the true pinnacle of excellence"*. The observation sums up the prevailing situation posed by the politics of ethnic identity divide in the NER, which the long term conflicts of the region have infused.

Because while the various major factions of the insurgent groups are busy negotiating peace with the government on one hand, some of them are covertly 'waging war' against the Indian state by means of the unconventional method of encouraging and inciting people belonging to their respective ethnic groups to advocate and espouse their cause. This 'proxy war', which tantamount to a symbolic assault on the country's integrity leads to ethnic tensions, conflicts and animosity adversely affecting the security scenario by disrupting public peace and order in the region. The various political parties are not averse to exploiting this situation.

It is the direction in which ethnic identity assertions that have taken ever since insurgency and militancy began in the NER, which is certainly a cause of concern and worry for all, especially for the government. It is the inability of the government to appreciate this aspect that assertive ethnic identity politics in the NER have; its ability to be in a way, a force multiplier for perpetuating the conflict situation started by the insurgency movements, which needs to be appropriately addressed on priority. One can assume that this lack of appreciation has greatly handicapped the security forces in handling the law and order problems in the region effectively. It is important to appreciate and understand these co-relationships.

Peace Negotiations

The third direct adverse impact of the prolonged insurgencies in the region is linked with law and order. This is partly due to the interpolative nature of identity politics which has permeated into every aspect of life in the region ever since it has emerged in the scene. The infusion of ethnic identity politics with the insurgent movements has removed the thin wedge that divided insurgency politics from the purely civilian ones. The interpolative nature of these two; ethnic identity and insurgency movements has resulted in creating an atmosphere of suspicion and acrimony across the NER. And since identity necessarily translates into real estate or geographical spaces the main source of livelihood for the people over which people would like to control, the peace negotiations between the government and some of the major insurgent groups are watched with apprehensions by all ethnic groups. Part of the reason no doubt is the nature and composition of the peace negotiations themselves, but most significantly the politics of identity over the years has come to be seen and linked with the question of title and ownership over land and territory. Consequently, the on-going peace negotiations and the existing accords themselves, which are restricted to only a few ethnic groups have within them the seeds of their own destructions as these do not completely address the concerns of all ethnic groups about their' titles over lands and territories.

This is mainly because the peace negotiations being undertaken between the Government and some of the major insurgent (ethnic) groups are bipartite in their format and approach and because of which most of the less vocal and less belligerent ethnic groups, who constitute the main peace-constituency in the NER feel being left out in the whole peace parleys. Part of the problem is that members of this 'peace constituency' are neither part of the peace-process nor are they made to feel that their apprehensions, concerns and anxieties particularly about their lands and territories are being taken care of in the peace parleys between Government and the insurgent groups. In due course, the members of this 'peace constituency' slowly get entrapped into the cauldron of ethnic identity assertions just like others in the NER and come out openly in defiance against the state.

Section II

Having identified assertive identity politics as one of the main causes for the perpetuations of the violence in the region one needs to analyses how these three problem areas can be overcome.

Development & Economic Well-Being as Panacea

One of the main causes of insurgency and the social unrest unleashed by the ethnic identity conflict and divide in the NER is additionally fueled by the continued preoccupation of the government with security of the region and trying to solve the problems of insurgency as well as the growing ethnic identity divide by deploying security forces more intensively as well as extensively in the NER, while simultaneously not doing enough to address the problems of poverty and underdevelopment of the region. The rather hesitant efforts, in fits and starts of the various economic development activities most often seen as knee-jerk responses in the past, has been one of the main reasons why people in the region get disillusioned and why the insurgent movements continue to find sympathisers and find popular support. The end result is that peace has been elusive. While one appreciates the dilemma the government faces of whether peace should precede development or the other way round, it should remember that while ideology fired the imaginations of the various insurgent leaders in the initial stages of their movements, however, over the years this has been replaced by the growing demand and need of the people to improve their material and economic well-being.

The preoccupation with security while understandable as such, it is vital and imperative for the government to make a deliberate shift in its tempo on the economic development of the region, by making a distinct departure from the general lack of enthusiasm that marked the earlier phases. Such an approach can certainly bring about changes in the attitude and the mind-set of people in the region. While skeptics fear that such a shift, which gets translated into transfers of huge finances and funds to the region would only enrich the militants' coffers and perpetuate insurgency in the process, there are also many others who contrary to this view believe that economic development and sincere efforts to enhance the well-being of the people side by side with the enforcement of law and order can have positive effects. The latter group believes that such a shift in emphasis can replace the peoples' preoccupation with identity politics. Such a change can be crucial and vital especially if government is serious about finding ways to win over the people of the region. Government has to move away from the oft repeated clichés of purpose and action of the past.

A shift in emphasis to address the economic and development needs of people in the region can not only wean away people from their preoccupation with their ethnic identities, but simultaneously, if this is combined with government's efforts also to down play the security oriented approach in solving the problems of the region, a much more conducive environment can be created in which peace stands a better chance to survive. Such an approach for a region like the NER is all the more necessary today than it ever was. In fact today we live in a world where the once politically and spatially defined contours and political boundaries of nations, not to speak of states are getting redefined by the czars of the industrial world who undertake investment decisions and can change the face of a region like the NER. These non-state players conceive and work in a world order where the politically 'divided' national boundaries are slowly getting superimposed by an economical one. In such a situation when national boundaries and their restrictive mandate are getting blunted, the boundaries among states within a country, metaphorically speaking should also slowly become less and less relevant both territorially as well as psychologically at least among the constituent citizens of the country and the NER. The states in the NER cannot exist in 'splendid isolation' as they had done in the past by trying to define themselves as separate small silos of exclusivity, at least developmentally and economically as such. They must instead find ways and means to come closer together by thinking developmentally for economic prosperity and shifting their priorities from their preoccupation with divisive identity politics to one of cooperation and partnership among themselves.

These changes have a profound impact and implication for the peripheral regions like the Northeast, which has so far depended largely only on the largess of the Government. This is because whatever little funds that flow as private investments into the NER can also dry up as the chances for reverse outflows of funds from the region to other regions, which possess and provides better investment opportunities and facilities than the NER can take place. In such a changed economic world order, regions like the NER becomes extremely vulnerable to neglect and commensurate decay. Something needs to be done.

In the overall analyses, a paradigm shift in thinking is called for to both counter the threats posed by the globalization process sweeping the country and simultaneously also to take advantage of the opportunity that globalization can provide to the Northeast region. It is in this context that as stakeholders, all the member states of the NER must rethink and learn to adjust themselves and think as a group for economic development instead of preoccupying themselves with the identity politics they have overwhelmed themselves with. The idea of constituting and thinking of themselves as one single economic bloc without in any manner diluting or disturbing the existing political setup and administrative arrangements can be pursued. From this perspective, there is an urgent need to overcome the unfortunate prevailing atmosphere of mistrust and acrimonious equations among the people and states in the region.

Law and Order

The adverse effect conspicuously marked by the changes in ethnic relationships observed earlier due to the long-term prevalence of insurgency and the commensurate related violence in the NER today poses as one of the most serious challenges to the NER and the country today. This change in the profile and character of insurgency and its effect on ethnic identity relationships has blurred the distinctions between the two types of law and order problems; the one that concerns a threat to the unity and sovereignty of the nation directly, and those which are largely defined as internal domestic law and order problems, which does not challenge the authority of the state or country. Because of this change, efficacy and effectiveness of several legislations meant to enable the administration as well as the security forces in the region to handle the various law and order problems have largely been nullified or neutralized.

The indistinct nature of law and order situation has created a piquant situation complicating the already complex law and order situation in the region. The net result is that the security forces who are expected to handle and deal with the given situation quite often end-up inappropriately handling the situations either by using too much or too little force, attracting public criticism and anger either way. This is a major challenge to the administration and the security forces in the NER. On the contrary, because of this piquant situation some of the legislations like the Armed Forces (Special Powers) Act of 1958, meant to enable the security forces to tackle the problems of insurgency effectively, have instead become the cause of public anger and criticism. These pose one of the greatest challenges to the government and the various law enforcement agencies.

In this connection in an interesting analysis the former Judge Advocate General (JAG) of the Indian Army, Major General Nilendra Kumar, (Retd) had made a suggestion that there is a need to educate and connect the personnel of the security forces about the environment, the various subtle nuances of the socio-political aspects of the people amidst whom they are expected to, or being deployed. Implied in this observation and suggestion is the fact that there is a degree of inadequacy in the training being imparted to the security forces being deployed in these sensitive areas like the NER.

The suggestion is interesting, because by the very command-structure of the armed forces while senior level officers are familiarised and acquainted with the various issues and problems of the environment they are engaged, in the lower levels of the command-structure there is a lack of adequate understanding about various issues and aspects of the people and the region they are expected to work in. This greatly handicaps the commanders and men; especially people on the action-spots, to appreciate the subtle nuances and sensitivities involved to enable them to correctly apply the degree or level of force to be deployed and in determining the general appropriateness of the manner and form that needs to be used. The extent of knowledge suggested here is essentially the need to familiarise and facilitate these commanders and their men to have a correct and proper appraisal of the social and civil 'equations' among the various peoples living in the area of 'operation' so that in the process they do not unnecessarily attract public criticism of the kind one has seen in very recent times. The attempt is to preempt the unfortunate usage of either too much or too little force by them or prevent the targeting the wrong set of people.

The Peace Paradigm: Need for Recontextualisation

The general law and order situation in the NER has changed in recent times due to enervation and the stubborn refusal of the GoI to negotiate on any aspect relating to sovereignty and integrity of the country. Additionally, the decisions to provide separate political spaces and autonomy to a few major upland tribal communities have dented the severity and extent of insurgent movements. All these efforts are reflected in the reduced number of insurgency related cases from the region. However, in spite of these positive developments stalemate continues in many of peace efforts.

This is because 'peace' in its present form and format in the NER means different things to different ethnic identities. This is primarily because 'peace' being negotiated is seen by most ethnic groups as one between government and one insurgent (ethnic) group, not necessarily one that guarantees to each of them with the prospect of their concerns and apprehensions being appropriately factored in or being addressed. This leaves the on-going peace process highly unacceptable to most people of the region. Implicit in this observation is the suspicion that the ongoing peace processes do not give the confidence and assurances that all the ethnic groups in the region hope or expect to get. Seen from this perspective, it is evident that the peace process and the peace-accords in their present form and content may not be able to provide the kind of peace the people of the NER as a whole would like to have.

Given this scenario, there is need to redefine peace and evolve a new approach to the peace-making process in the context of the NER so that people of the region can relate to it much more meaningfully than it is done today. Once the peace-processes are made transparent and made generally acceptable across the ethnic divide in the NER, durable peace is distinctly possible. It is in this context it is vital that any peace effort in the NER must be made adequately comprehensive and inclusive enough to address the concerns of all ethnic groups of the region if durable peace has to find a place in the NER.

It is important to realize this aspect of the peace process because all the ethnic groups will be affected one way or the other sooner or later as they will have to live side by side. It is in this context that the terms and conditions of the peace accords irrespective of the insurgent groups involved becomes vital to each one of them. The basic inherent fears of being forced into a situational *fait-accompli* remain the weakest point in the ongoing peace negotiations cutting across ethnic lines in the region. Realizing this is vital in formulating any peace plan for the NER, especially if it has to succeed. Even if these factors might have been considered in the past very little has been done to espouse the confidence and assurances to the various ethnic groups who are not active parties in the peace making process. Failure to show and assure the people the fact that these issues have been and are being addressed can be a major source of the problem to the peace-making process. Given the prevailing approach the on-going dialogues and the peace making process somehow appear incomplete and quite inadequate.

The NER needs a peace process that addresses these issues holistically. Peace in the context of the NER therefore has to be comprehensive, regional in content and in context emphasizing its role as means to bridge the ethnic divide. To reiterate, peace, durable peace in the context of the NER must create a set of unique value, capable of addressing and assuaging the psychological anxieties and fears of all concerned. To achieve this government needs to choose a different path quite distinct from what has already been tried in the past.

The Need to Shift Emphasis

The fact that insurgency in the NER is directly linked to the ethnic identity politics is by now well established. The fact also that this unfortunate phenomenon has been in a way 'imposed' on the people of the region by factors and circumstances of history that were beyond their control makes it relevant to explore if the adverse impact of its influence can be stalled if not completely reversed.

In this connection in a fundamentally distinct findings of researches undertaken by a few social scientists on people from the Himalayan region in Nepal has found that people from these areas (by implication similar to areas like the Northeast) even after they have migrated and left their native places for work outside the region, still continue to retain their deep bond to people and places of their birth. It has also been found that this bonding and affiliation is in spite of the fact that most of the people they grew up with were not necessarily people belonging to their respective or particular ethnic group. It was found that this bonding persisted primarily because they were born and brought up in a particular place and among a particular set of people. These researches establish the fascinating and interesting fact that this notion of 'belonging' that people have for a particular place and people, commands a distinct and an unique bond of feelings and camaraderie that go much deeper than the mere cataloging of people by their ethnic identities affinities. These findings provide an entirely new perspective from which the ethnic identity, especially in the context of the NER can be analysed, by shifting the emphasis from the conventionally accepted notion that human bondings and relationships are necessarily based on primarily because of their ethnic identity relationships. The research provides a whole new way of dealing and looking at ethnic identity politics of the NER. It also provides a new perspective and means by which people of diverse ethnicities and groups can come closer together even if they are not linked by ancestral or blood relationships as a group.

Viewed from this perspective ethnic identity (which predominate the polity of the NER) tend to be what many social scientists describe as essentially a political construct, one that evolved over centuries when people, especially those belonging to smaller ethnic groups formed such a construction and formed associations to constitute into a group to forge a security cover to fortify themselves against their larger detractors or enemies. Thus while ethnic identity reflects the socio-political side and meet the immediate physical needs as a group, the notion of 'belonging' reflects and addresses the more innate, emotional and psychological side of peoples' deeper and private feelings through their individual private and subjective 'experiences'. In a way therefore, the notion of 'belonging' and by implications its various derivatives can be an alternative to ethnic identity affiliations. It is arguably most likely to be 'acceptable' as a way to identify people in the NER along with and in addition to being identified by their ethnic identities. This is primarily because the relationship 'forged' through the notion of 'belonging' is less obtrusive and do not bear the definitive arrogance that the socio-politically constructed concept of ethnic identity denotes or implies. In the context of the NER, it may be desirable to highlight this qualitative difference and looking and dealing with human relationships in the region beyond the confines of ethnic identity divide. The notion of 'belonging' can therefore be a new value-proposition which can be highlighted more and more.

In short, the notion of 'belonging' if stressed and understood in the proper and correct perspective by the people of the NER, a new basis and approach to human relationships between the indigenous groups of people and those born in these societies can be defined. It provides a distinct way for sobering and mellowing down the angst and animosity that indigenous people have against 'others'; non-indigenous people who do not ethnically or racially belong to the various anthropological groups from the NER. Once this aspect is appreciated and realised, the chances of changes in the thinking and attitude of people about themselves and of others in the troubled NER becomes much more realizable. For the government and the people of the region by therefore highlighting and shifting the focus of human relationships to the notion of 'belonging', the 'softer' side of peoples' experiences and associations, an alternative way to deal with the problem of ethnic relationships may perhaps be able to be found.

Section III

Long term Impact: The Great National Prejudice

Even though the consequences of the longterm conflicts is being analysed with reference to the NER specifically, a few observations are inevitably necessary when dealing with the subject as vast and wide as the present one from the national perspective.

Today the number of insurgency related deaths in the NER is far less than ever, with almost the entire region free from insurgency except for occasional skirmishes and violence that takes place once in a while that too in one or two states. Simultaneously, various peace negotiations are on between government and some insurgent groups. The old war-horses, the straight-jacketed ideologues who inspired and were the source of inspirations of the various movements have yielded places to the younger generation, and in the process a 'shift' in thinking and attitude is noticed. All these have changed the peace environment in the region. Yet the national prejudice that the NER continues to be totally under the grip of 'anarchy' and 'mayhem' and that nothing progressive or developmental can be done continues to grip the national mindset. In this connection many commentators have observed on several occasions that there are more deaths on the streets of any one of our major cities in India daily and annually, than the number of insurgency related deaths in the NER.

This 'impression' about people and the NER that has got so deeply ingrained (or made to be ingrained by ill-informed and inadequate dissemination of news and views) in the minds of people across the country that people from the NER now interpret this 'attitude' as a good national 'ploy' and an excuse, an alibi for the country not to do anything substantial developmentally and economically as much for the region as the government should. Many people in the NER see this 'attitude' being reflected from the general reluctance to invest in the region to the tendency of government officials trying to avoid postings in the NER. It is a sad commentary and reflection on our national character.

The situation is ironical because paradoxically, people in the NER seem to move on with their lives as in other part or region of the country. Part of the national prejudice is due to the historical legacy the region has inherited from the various insurgent movements that has taken place in the past. And to a large measure also from the fact that nothing positive or constructive has been done by the government to bring about a change in this thinking and attitude by highlighting the changing profile of the region. For some strange logic of perception we still love to treat the NER and its problems as an anthropological 'reserve'; perpetuating in the process the cult of the 'land of the head-hunters'.

In this given scenario, people from the NER tend to believe that as a nation we Indians have come to rationalise ourselves into believing that the NER is doomed to 'remain' inflicted by the scourge of insurgency and backwardness. There is a general apprehension, a psychosis that has gripped the country's perceptions and thinking about the people of the NER. Obviously, the long term impact of this 'perception' has left its tell-tale impact on the minds of people by conditioning them to think negatively about people and the region. This has affected the NER in several important areas especially in the investment and economic development sectors. As a consequence in the long term, self-doubt and uncertainty prevail in the minds of people of the region about their ability to overcome the problems of the region. These issues collectively erode the national confidence as a country.

As a sympathiser and a person from the NER one sees a certain amount of unfairness therefore in pronouncing the terminal 'tragic death' of the region by the country uncharitably. This is unfair mainly because the kind of appellative and the general impression people in the country have about the NER, which to say sadly is unfortunately based more on perceptions and hearsays than what it is in reality, destroys the hope of the people of the region to regenerate themselves and be part of the national building process. The observation once made jokingly and meant to be a sarcastic comment on those who believed that the NER was in a perpetual state of turmoil of people dying, popping off literally like pop-corns in every corner and part of the NER seems to linger on irrespective. Time has come to help and to correct the national perception. This aspect is certainly one of the most profound adverse consequences of the long-term conflict on the region.

This observation seems necessary because as one goes around in the NER, life here in the region seems to go on normally for the people irrespective and in spite of what is being said or observed or happening. And yet there is a tinge of sadness that lurks in the minds of people everywhere in the region; hamstrung by a perennial question of 'where do they go from here and how from now onwards'?. This question arises because the national 'prejudice' against them, by singling them out as a region perennially doomed to 'chaos', underdevelopment and mayhem saps their inner most strength to overcome their misfortune. The nation by their misinformed attitude is not helping in any way the people of the NER to over the plight. People in the NER therefore get the general impression that the neglect of the region is but a national alibi; a national excuse for people who matter to only perpetuate the 'neglect' that has marked the fate of the region since independence. Is this an imagined persecution complex the people of the NER suffer from?

Is it then that the NER is a region only where the armed and security forces are made to step in? A negative construction and meaning being seen and read in all these unfortunate situations is but natural. The impossible becomes possible, anything can be imagined and thought of, so also can the impressions that the negative image about the region that prevails in the country is also hyped up by vested interests and people. Similarly, violence can also be so tutored and its meanings manipulated for other selfish reasons even though the nature of violence itself cannot be modified. The tragedy is that today we the people in India generally (even though a distinction between the well informed and the general public seems desirable yet one refrains from doing so for very many obvious reasons) fall into this trap, and have gone more by impressions and hearsays than based on informed sources on the real situation and conditions that prevail in the NER today.

This observation it must be qualified however, as stated earlier is not to mean that even occasional insurgency related violence does not take place, but to mean that insurgency related violence is certainly not in the volume and proportion of what it has been made out or has been projected to be, at least in the last few years. It is the hype and the fear psychosis that has been woven around the myriad tales about the NER, which needs to be corrected. The country must ask the pertinent question of whether the negative impression or the fear psychosis that has been built around the NER and being attributed to insurgency is in national interests?

The above observation arises because one feels that peace and progress cannot be the monopoly of the rest of the country by leaving out the people of the NER alone. Just because there are a few insurgency related cases reported, we are not justified in condemning the people of the NER to live in a state of perpetual neglect and indifference they are in. We as a country seem to have lost our sense of perspective and balance. A time has come when our exaggerated sense of danger that we have built about the NER over the years need to be changed. The paper examines and analyses some of these issues.

Conclusion

The cyclic occurrences of violence that take place are rare and few these days and yet the consequences of the long term conflicts, essentially a historical legacy the region has inherited over the years and the stigma associated still remain. Thus today in spite of the changed and much improved law and order conditions in the NER we still speak or talk of insurgency and its related issues as if the problems remains as they were; both in their intensity and in their spread. And subsumed in this observation is the notion that insurgency can never be overcome in the NER. A cynic may have their views but one is not too carried away by their perceptions, understandings or logic of their appreciations of the problems of the NER. Instead one tends to believe that things are changing and will change further for the better, because the situation is capable of changing on its own esteem with a few nudging. The remedies suggested and the ways to look and deal with the situation may not be the ultimate answers to the various vexed problems but certainly nothing prevents from making a beginning on the new lines suggested.

In this connection one also believes that peace has always been intended to be achieved, but never fructified because of the lack of knowledge and understanding of the real issues and problems that trouble the people of the NER. A few of them have been discussed. Yet in each of these problems one sees also the seeds of 'hope' within each. Is economic development one such answer? It certainly cannot be the only answer and yet one is convinced that the economic prosperity and wellbeing of the people of the region has a tremendous and important role and part to play in the rehabilitation process, whether one may like it or not. Personally, I am convinced that the strongest antidote to insurgency is to take poverty and underdevelopment of the region heads-on, not in the half hearted patronising blend of 'empathy' and 'understanding' that New Delhi has exhibited in the last sixty years after independence. What is needed instead is sincerity of purpose, which many describe as the need for the desired 'political will'. Once the patronising arrogance of 'we know everything' is temporarily shelved by those who matter in the policy making hierarchy, and economic development is combined by changing the policy paradigm from the security perspective to one that aims at the wellbeing of the people, a possible way out of the problems of the region can be hoped for.

Simultaneously, it must be emphasised that in all these developments all the ethnic groups of the region have to shift their focus from their monomaniacal preoccupation with their respective ethnic identities by trying to see human relationships from the prisms of what has been described as the more acceptable notion of 'belonging'. As the ethnic fabric of the region has been soiled and made sullied over the last sixty years in the region by several unfortunate decisions and events a change in focus and approach is felt can necessary to redeem the NER from where it has fallen into.

The perspective from which one has analysed the consequences of the long term impact of conflicts in the NER as one essentially a problem of the people and the region is unrealistic in many ways than one. For one, from this perspective one seems to have very conveniently forgotten the long term impact of the 'calamity' that has befallen the NER is also a national problem that has adversely affects and sullies the image of India as a nation and a democracy in the eyes of the world.

As a nation, appreciating the problem of the NER from this perspective is significant because the prevalence of the conflicts in the NER over the years in a strange but real way, demoralises (albeit sub-consciously if not openly) all Indians as it questions of our faith in our ability to manage the affairs of the nation, especially of our inability to deal with problems of a small part of our vast country. This fact in spite of all the rich legacy of our history makes our claims to greatness appear hollow. It demolishes our own self-esteem.

The people and country must not therefore forget that the so called impact of the long term conflict in the NER described in all its candidness and truthfulness is a shame on all of us; Indians for allowing the NER to be what it is. The situation in the NER is not to be seen and treated as has been often seen and described as a 'shame' for the people of the NER alone, but as a national problem, a gnawing reminder to each and every Indian to do much more to put things right in its own backyard. In short, the people of the NER needs a healing phase in its history that unites rather than divides the people of the region.

Impact on Nagaland and Naga Affairs

Monalisa Changkija

Conflict in the Northeast is generally perceived from the prism of insurgency and militancy and worse still, it appears that such conflicts are perceived to exist in a vacuum or in isolation from the various other conflicts that not only create insurgency and militancy but also those that are created by insurgency and militancy. I would like to underscore that the commonly believed conflicts created by insurgency and militancy are only a part of the larger conflicts confronting the Northeast and it is these larger conflicts that pose perhaps greater challenges, threats and risks to the region.

Let us appreciate that Northeastern societies were in existence centuries before the rise of some conflicts such as insurgency and militancy. In fact, these are recent developments, not even a century old. Older conflicts relating to histories, ideologies, politics, cultures, traditions, religions, beliefs, superstitions, lore and legends of primarily tribal societies are harder to deal with, especially through and with modern concepts such as democracy and institutions thereof, which are of the alien variety, unmindfully imposed post-Independence, on ancient societies with developed semblances of democratic concepts and practices. So when we talk about conflict in the Northeast and the concomitant challenges, threats and risks, we have to understand, appreciate and discern the kinds of conflicts that confront the region.

Besides the usual conflicts that insurgency and militancy pose to any society in any part of the globe, perhaps what is often forgotten, ignored and demeaned are the conflicts entrenched in tribalism, conflicting aspirations and interests, cultural diversities and dreams and schemes of tribal hegemony, as also power struggles at varied and various levels of society, perhaps due to multiplicity of value-systems we subscribe to in our society, especially keeping in mind that these are the very same factors that also spawn insurgency and militancy. This, of course, we would be able to understand

and appreciate better if we keep in mind the historical fact that not only have tribal societies in the Northeast, especially Naga society, been rudely tossed from our subsistence economies into modern forms of economies but also the fact that our histories and cultures were unceremoniously hijacked at a certain point of time by alien forces and factors. This has disoriented us and this disorientation has spawned conflicts that have hitherto been ignored, neglected or simply brushed off as extraneous to the larger scheme of things of matters Northeast. What needs to be underscored here is the fact that standing at the crossroads of the traditional and modernity, Northeastern societies are not very sure as to how to view and what to make out of the rapidly-changing equations we see all around us, locally, regionally, nationally and globally. And when one is not sure of things, one tends to look at them with suspicion, with fear and retreat into a kind of passivity.

The entrenched impact of such a situation is not easy to discern; so what is needed is an in-depth study of the psychological profiles of our peoples, which have shaped our histories, economies, politics, cultures, traditions, laws, lore and legends, keeping in mind that over the centuries, these very same factors have also shaped our psychological profiles. The interesting aspect of it all is that the present Northeastern societies may be a result of western or modern orientation by way of education and the technological revolution increasingly reaching our remotest areas but our people are also products of deep-seated traditional cultures and concepts. We also need to deal with our inability and/or unwillingness to shed our biases and prejudices, and our traditional and cultural viewpoints of the world in general. Consequently, we have sidelined and unwittingly imprisoned ourselves to the 'dominant' politics, economics, cultures, ideologies, and what is made out to be the 'dominant aspirations' of our peoples. This perhaps ranks as one of the greatest 'conflicts' that rage in Northeastern societies. The worst fallout of this is the violation of all human democratic rights and freedoms. The fallout incidentally is in harmony with the tribal principle that the collective is greater than the individual – a principle that had helped overground political classes and underground factions to silence the people.

The primary challenge hence is to find ways and means to help our people focus on and understand the numerous issues and dimensions of our varied and various conflicts, find our own answers and solutions and find a common platform to address conflicting issues. But the problem is our conflicts keep us divided and as we have experienced, any attempt to build such platforms are hijacked by forces that do not see their interests being served by such bridging and unifying platforms. We have also experienced that tribal bodies are not the answer.

As an example, I would like to underscore the issue of the 33 per cent reservation for women in urban bodies, which the Nagaland State Assembly passed in 2006. Tribal bodies have vehemently opposed this on the ground that traditionally Naga women are not allowed participation in the decision making process, which is true. The male-only tribal bodies quote Article 371 (A) of the Indian Constitution, which protects Naga Customary Laws. However, our male-only tribal bodies refuse to concede that urban bodies such as municipal councils, town committees, etc., are not Naga traditional decision making bodies but constitutional bodies which cannot bar women from entry and participation. Here, by and large, our political parties tacitly support the male-only tribal bodies because they see Naga women's entry into the constitutional political process as a threat to their political careers as Naga women have today educationally and in every other way outpaced Naga men although political parties may issue press statements from time to time to demand that the State Government implement the 33 per cent women's reservation, which is basically a paper war between rival political parties, not any concern for women's political empowerment. Anyway, Naga women took the issue of the 33 per cent reservation for women in urban bodies to the Guwahati High Court, which unfortunately sided with the opinion of our male-only tribal bodies as also our male-only state Legislative Assembly, both of which are in total agreement on barring women from the decision making process. Of course, now the case has been taken to the Supreme Court and its judgment is awaited.

The point here is that any society that is governed both by archaic, undemocratic and unrepresentative Customary Laws and simultaneously by the well-defined Constitution of the world's largest democracy is bound to create confusion and conflicts, especially because our Constitution actually protects and preserves these archaic, undemocratic and unrepresentative Customary Laws. And not just in the matter of women's participation in the decision making process but also in all other aspects of societal life, for instance marital problems, land disputes, etc. This creates the space and the scope for all kinds of elements to fish in troubled waters. Because our Justice delivery system is not as efficient and effective as we would like it to be, issues are either taken up to political personalities or underground factions for reddressal, and these entities use such 'cases' to impose and perpetuate their 'power', which further subjugates and dis-empowers the ordinary citizen. The loser often goes to the rival political party personalities and/or the rival underground faction – the cycle get more vicious. In brief, a tensed situation is created resulting in multi-dimension conflicts involving the traditional and the modern. These cycles and circles of conflicts then get more accentuated and this cannot be resolved by the Armed Forces (Special) Powers Act or any similar draconian Act to "contain" insurgency.

As regards Nagaland particularly, I am of the opinion that our conflicts began with our migration or it is possible that conflicts in the places of our origin have led to our migration and we carried the conflicts with us. I do not speak with any authority on the matter but by trying to understand the age-old affinity or animosity individual Naga tribes or groups of Naga tribes have with each other till now. Apparently, there have been different waves of migration of the Naga tribes and some of the tribes seem to have migrated together or within short spans of time leading to either affinity or animosity. This affinity or animosity still exists in one form or the other, especially in the form of our age-old land and boundary disputes, which have cost precious lives. Evidence also lie in the modern formation of groups under the umbrella of a dominant tribe, for instance the Tenyimei group of about six tribes, the group of about seven tribes under the umbrella of the Eastern Naga Peoples' Organization (ENPO), which is demanding for a separate "Frontier Nagaland" state. Recently, four tribes of central Nagaland, namely the Ao, Lotha, Sema and Rengma tribes, have formed another group. Also, evidence lie in the modern political formation such as political parties and the same can be seen in the composition of underground factions.

It is often believed that the Naga national movement has shaped the political thinking of the Nagas say, since the late 1920s, but in my opinion it is the thinking of traditional Naga mind that has shaped the Naga national movement. The traditional Naga thinking was that we were always sovereign hence we should always remain sovereign. This can be best understood only if we know the character, contents and composition, as also the status and dynamics of the Naga village. Traditionally, each Naga village was totally sovereign and no over-all tribal body existed with any control over any individual Naga village – none exist even now. The village authority, in the form of village parliaments, was the final sovereign body, which were democratic in nature, except for two tribes that had hereditary king-ships. No doubt, in the past twenty years or so, individual tribal bodies have been formed and their representatives form the Naga Hoho but they are basically NGOs or civil societies with the primary objective of maintaining cultural and social cooperation, maintaining harmony and good will amongst the various Naga tribes and non-Naga communities in Nagaland, etc. Their brief clearly is to act as bridges of amity amongst the population of the state. They do not have any political mandate but have assumed political character over the years as they are patronised by overground political parties and personalities as well as underground factions. As a natural corollary, these Hohos have come to believe that they have the people's 'mandate'. As you are well aware, another player, in the form of these tribal Hohos, has stepped into our muddied waters, muddying it even more. Anyway, suffice it to say here that 'sovereignty' is deeply-rooted in our psyche and is an integral part of our tradition and culture. And it is from this perspective we must understand Nagas' fascination with sovereignty.

Now a broad example of Ao Naga village governance: "The Ao tribe has three different types of traditional institutions such as the *Putu Menden* (generation rule) among the Chungli group, the *Samen Menchen* (meat share rule) among the Mongsen group and the *Yanga Samen* (age-set system rule), which is also called the *Samen Menchen*. The village polity and distribution of power is determined by type of traditional institution that is followed. The Mongsen group follows the system of government whereby the founding clans of the village occupy the top most positions and are in power for ten to fifteen years after which younger people take over. Among the Chungli group, the Putu Menden system of government is followed wherein a number of age-set grades are clubbed together into one 'generation'. A father and his son cannot be of the same 'generation'.

There are five such 'generations' and each of them rule for twenty to twenty-five years (tenure differs from village to village). In this system too, the clans occupy top positions. There is another system of governance based purely on the age-set system found in Changki and Khar villages in the Changkikong Range, wherein the age-set grades move up progressively every three to five years and when they reach the traditionally prescribed grade to be in the village government, the members are automatically inducted into the village government regardless of whether they belong to the founding clan or not.

"In the *Putu Menden* (Chungli) and the *Samen Menchen* (Mongsen) there is a clear distinction between the founding clans and the clans that settled later, who are also known as 'latecomers'. The founding clans hold all the powers while later settlers are relegated to the lower ranks. However in the Yanga (age-set) system, there are no such distinctions and each person gets to be in the village government regardless of whether he belongs to the founding clan or not..."[1]

Unfortunately, the Industrial Revolution and all that happened after that led to the creation of nation states and changed the meaning of sovereignty across the world and small societies like us had no chance, not to mention choice. Therein hangs a tale of one of our conflicts. And this tale carries on with both the Government of India and the Nagaland government finding themselves unable to deal with the multi-faceted roadblocks they confront in dealing with our political, economic and social issues. Meanwhile, our underground factions too are confronted with the traditional Naga thinking that doesn't quite subscribe to submissiveness. Inarguably, the modern concepts of sovereignty, nation-state, etc., which require a good degree of submission will take time to penetrate deep into the Naga psyche.

Yes, besides the traditional affinities and animosities, we also need to deal with the entire concept of the nation-state, the concepts of identity and ethnicity, etc., turning upside down as far as the Naga psyche is concerned. A prime example would be the events that have been happening in Changki

---

[1] Jungmayangla Longkumer, *Change and Continuity in Tribal Villages: A Sociological Study*, (Akansha Publishing House: New Delhi, 2009)

Village of Mokokchung district in the past few years, wherein attempts were made to make the tradition subservient to the modern thus creating another kind of conflict. A case in point is Changki Village saw the traditional and the modern merging to not very happy consequences. This is a very old village, established much before the Ahoms migrated to the Northeast and evidence still exist of Ahoms crossing through the village territory. The village was originally formed by ten clans, other clans came later. Head hunting and slavery was a part of the traditional Naga life so original Changki settlers captured one group, who were eventually allowed to be settled in the village in a given area under the village jurisdiction but they wanted to settle in the Changki Lower Khel, founded by the leader of the ten clans who migrated to the present site – in the heart of the seat of Village governance and power. Since this group had no traditional ancestral name, they were given the nomenclature Emremchangki, which loosely translated means "Attached to Changkiri clan" and they were allowed to settle inside the village on four conditions set by the Founding village leader. They were: (a) Since they would be attached to Changkiri clan (founding clan and the founding clan of the Changki Lower Khel), there will be no intermarriage amongst them; (b) Village subscriptions would be separate; (c) There would be no common inheritance amongst them; (d) Use of hereditary nomenclature would be separate.

For several centuries, peace reigned in Changki Village and the captured group, called the Emremchangki, had completely assimilated into the Changki community life. But trouble started when this group claimed to be of the Changkiri clan, which is a founding clan of the village. In Naga society, one cannot change the clan one is born into and the clan name cannot be given or appropriated by anyone not belonging to the clan. In Naga society, the clan name is sacrosanct. Further, this group also contested the issue of the founding clans. Our village customary tradition entitles the village council (seat of village governance) to collect citizenship/membership fees from every able-bodied males above the age of eighteen. The Emremchangki clan refused to pay this membership under their nomenclature. They insisted on paying only as members of the Changkiri clan. Since the village council refused to accept their claim, they stopped paying the citizenship/membership fees since the last ten to twelve years. As per Naga traditions and customs, those who do not pay their citizenship/membership fees have no right to live in the village and conduct normal community life. They have to leave the village. A directive to such effect was issued to the Emremchangki by the village council — some of them left the village for Mokokchung, some stayed back as they had no issue about being Emremchangki and asserted that they were not of the Changkiri clan. Thus the Emremchangki group was divided.

The group that left for Mokokchung went to court, which passed a judgment in their favour and unacceptable to the village authority. Arrest warrants were issued to Village council members, which they ignored. The Court could not or did not enforce its own judgment. The same group of Emremchangkis then lodged a complain with the Ao Region Isak-Muivah (IM), which summoned the three parties – the Village council, the Emremchangki, which stayed back in the village and those who went to Mokokchung. After listening to all the three parties the Ao region IM advised them to live in unity. The Mokokchung group of the Emremchangki then went to the Ao Senden (Ao Hoho), which is actually just an NGO and have no mandate to arbitrate over intra and/or inter village disputes. Still, the Ao Region IM and the Ao Senden tied up, allegedly after being paid a good sum of money, and expelled Changki village from the Ao community and the Ao Senden. The question is: can an NGO and/or an underground faction expel any village from any community within Naga society? Another question is: Do insurgent groups have any jurisdiction over traditional Naga village laws and customs, which are protected by Article 371 (A) of the Indian Constitution?

Here it must also be mentioned that education leading to economic prosperity, political power and social status have combined together as a factor for erstwhile captured groups to aspire to rise in the village hierarchy and seek the same status and power of the founding clans. It is no secret that the MLA from this village belongs to a national political party, which also has links to underground factions. So, it was but natural to seek the Ao Region IM to arbitrate over the issue.

The Changki Village Imbroglio, as it was known as, generated much debates and discussions and finally the Ao Senden requested the Changki village to rejoin the Ao Senden. Changki village accepted their invitation and rejoined it. The dissenting Emremchangki didn't like the amicable settlement between the Changki village and the Ao Senden. So when a new team of Ao Senden took up office after this settlement, the dissenting Emremchangkis approached them again to reopen the case. The new Ao Senden team refused, so once again they went to the Ao Region IM, which issued an azha (dictum) preventing any Changki villager from moving out of the village, banning all economic activities and blockading all roads to and from the village. In effect, the Changki villagers were imprisoned within the village area and prevented from going about their normal day-to-day activities, which adversely impacted the village economy and education of young people, as IM cadres had also stopped private and state buses in the Changki jurisdiction and stopped Changki villagers from travelling. How badly the village economy was affected can be best understood if we remember that almost all villagers are cultivators, who need to go down to their paddy fields from their hill-top villages. Changki villagers protested against the IM's azha by taking out a procession from the village to Mariani in Assam, a distance of over 40 kilometres, which the IM couldn't hinder or stop.

Reportedly, the Cease-Fire Monitoring Group (CFMG) has also come down heavily on the IM on the azha. Yes, there is simmering anger against the IM for this azha. Although there were and still are individuals who have joined or supported one or the other faction from the beginning, Changki village as a whole remained neutral politically. In the early days, when the Federal Government of Nagaland (FGN) tried to enter the village, they failed as villagers cordoned off the village peripheries and put up bungees. Prior to this, no head-hunter could enter this village, which has the record of not having any of its citizen's head hunted. For centuries, there is only one known record of a Changki head hunted, of a woman, which happened outside the village peripheries. But Changki villagers successfully hunted head and also captured large numbers of slaves.

Changki village also has never been attacked by the Indian Army throughout Nagaland's history of insurgency and counter-insurgency. In fact, since the 1950s, the Indian Army has set up a camp within the village area, firstly the 4/8 Gorkha Rifles, then the 1/8 Gorkha Rifles and now the Assam Rifles are posted to that Camp. There has also been no case of rape, molestation and other crimes against women by any personnel of the Indian Army posted to the camp at Changki village since the 1950s.

While, looking from the perspectives of the 21st century democratic ethos, perhaps Naga traditional customs and laws are 'primitive' and definitely patriarchal nevertheless, these customs and laws have kept villages sovereign, united, law-abiding, disciplined and contributory. The quality of village leadership has also impacted on the growth and development of the village and kept the village sovereign because how the village is governed is solely up to the wisdom of the leadership and this is unequivocally protected by Article 371 (A) of the Indian Constitution. However, when the rhythm of the village governance and community life is disturbed because of internal disagreements, differences and dissent or because of external factors and forces, sometimes invited by sections of the village, numerous types of conflicts get mixed up and normal life is adversely affected, which in turn creates the scope and space for newer kinds of conflicts. It may also be mentioned here that the example of Changki village is not an exception. There are numerous other villages across Nagaland that have internal disagreements, differences and dissent, which have become happy hunting grounds for both overground and underground politics.

I would like to underscore the multiplicity of systems of governance, both constitutional and non-state that has not only befuddled the Naga mind but also have created the space and scope for more conflicts, which all go towards aggravating a tensed situation further leading to alienation and marginalization of the individual Naga from being a productive member of society and state. In other words, the Naga individual is rendered a prey, hunted by numerous hunters, often invisible and in incomprehensible avatars. For an average villager anywhere in Nagaland, tribal Hohos and the state Government are merely lore and legends. For them, the underground factions are bogeys that actually prey on them but sometimes a necessary evil to quickly dispose off disputes, at a price of course.

Corruption is so rampant and so deeply entrenched that it is not always for political reason, people look up to underground factions to deliver justice, or what is believed to be justice. Added to this is the political class' greed for votes to gain power and/or to remain in power. The soil is perfect to grow a happy relationship between the underground factions and the political class – the currency of exchange for this relationship of course being the Indian Rupee, the helpless and hapless ordinary citizen seen solely as a voter, and arms. Now, could all this 'happy' development take place without the knowledge and complicity, one way or the other, of the bureaucrat? In Nagaland, sometimes the power of the bureaucrat is even greater than that of the political class or the underground, sometimes both put together. The bureaucrat, after all, prepares the planning budget and knows the ways how more Central funds can be accrued. Under these circumstances, rebellions and revolutions, which we sometimes call conflicts to be politically correct, are just waiting to happen. We have seen how Changki villagers had the courage to peacefully defy the IM's azha in a do-or-die manner. But can we guarantee that numerous simmering angers brewing across Nagaland for varied and various reasons against numerous factors and forces would always be peacefully courageous or courageously peaceful? Clearly then, the impact of these conflicts reduces the Naga individual to a handicapped, disabled, disturbed and a very baffled person, who does not know whom to believe, who to look up for leadership, where to seek solace and most importantly where to look for justice. Such persons also have the tendency to do the most unexpected, not always resulting in happy consequences. Such persons are also the most vulnerable therefore the perfect candidates to fall for false promises made by the unscrupulous amongst the overground political class, the underground factions and the middle-ground trouble-makers with pretensions to being 'public leaders'.

It is not surprising that there is an exodus of our young people to cities across the country and these young people have no intention of returning home. What would they return to? Yes, we are also telling our daughters not to return home for there is nothing for them here – you will understand if you take a cursory look at our Customary Laws related to women. For Naga women, it makes no difference whether we live under traditional village governance, under the Indian system of governance or whatever system the underground factions have in mind; our Customary Laws, protected under Article 371 (A) of the Indian Constitution, would still dictate women's lives and I see no chance of the Indian Government and the Indian people putting down their feet and doing away with what is patriarchally perceived as sacrosanct i.e. our Customary Laws related to women. No wonder even middle-aged Naga women dream of moving out. The first step has already been taken with the migration from our villages to our towns. This doesn't portend well if we really believe that women are the mainstay of a society and state's development. The issue of the 33 per cent reservation for women in our urban bodies have already been explained, albeit briefly. Because the Naga women are denied and deprived of an identity, property and a place in society and state under our Customary Laws, they also form a segment of our floating population, which can go out of control keeping in mind issues of the flesh trade, substance and alcohol abuse, HIV/AIDS and numerous other very frightening issues, which are not only consequences of various kinds of conflicts but also causes of numerous types of conflicts already rearing their ugly heads. In the past few years, women have been nabbed not only for smuggling drugs but also for smuggling guns. This, I suspect, has more to do with economic reasons than for any ideological and political reasons – just a cursory study of the economic and educational status of women found involved in such activities reveal that. Although women were persuaded to believe that for beauty, customs were made to tattoo them in Northeastern traditional tribal societies, it is a well known fact that women were tattooed to keep raiders and head-hunters away from villagers that had beautiful women. The question is: are today's Naga women going to be 'tattooed' all over again just to keep 'raiders' and head-hunters', in the form of numerous conflicts, afflicting our society and state?

It is against these backgrounds, we must look at the Look East Policy (LEP). In fact, we must look at the whole issue of governance, economic, political and security policies, funds, funding patterns and absence of supervision and monitoring thereof, etc., that are believed to be beneficial for the development of the people and state of Nagaland. We understand that at the time of Independence, India's focus was undividedly towards its western border but that still doesn't explain why even one or two good men or women couldn't have been spared to focus some attention towards our part of the country, which was over-ran by battalions and brigades of the Indian Armed Forces. If right from the time of Independence, some attention was paid towards the Northeast, particularly Nagaland for obvious historical reasons, the contagion of conflict may never have afflicted the entire region. The focus now should be towards making up for lost time, not only to resolve conflicts caused by insurgency and militancy but to resolve core conflicts that cause insurgencies and militancy.

While much have been said and written about the Look East Policy, we still do not know what it says exactly and how the Northeastern region could be pivotal to the Policy, for its own sake, except for the impression we get that our region would be the main transportation route through which Corporate India would conduct trade and commerce with our Eastern neighbours. Transportation routes, as we know, are no-man's land and in time even the indigenous people, who own such land, get disowned for transportations routes for trade and commerce tend to get insidiously proprietary. Unless the Look East Policy is unambiguously spelt out, there is much scope for social upheavals in this regions, especially as trade and commerce, or let us say that the whole process of globalization and its concomitants, begin a disintegrating process of the value-systems and cultures of the region, as we have seen happening is so many parts of the globe. We are seeing what is happening in China and Russia in the name of economic development and globalization, the rot has already set in India too – can we now afford this very vulnerable region to undergo the same process if the Look East Policy is not clearly spelled out, supervised and monitored? Some may opine that the rot has already set in, in the Northeast region beginning with the export of insurgency from Nagaland. But could this have been possible without the unhindered scope for drug and arms trade in the region? How does the Look East Policy propose to contain, if not stop, this very lucrative drugs and arms 'trade and commerce', which fuels conflicts and create newer ones?

How and with what does the Look East Policy propose to pay the environmental price this region would indubitably pay, as infrastructure development becomes the primary development mantra of the Central Government in the Northeast? Considering that this region is almost inaccessible to foreigners and other citizens of the country in the form of Inner Line Permits, Restricted Area Permits, etc., can trade and commerce be expected to be robust without the intermingling of those involved in it, so how does the Look East Policy propose to reconcile protectionism and globalization? More importantly, what does the Look East Policy have for our educated young people, who have already gone outside the state and the region looking for, and finding, greener pastures elsewhere? Would the Look East Policy offer a much greener pasture to reverse the brain drain from Nagaland? These and several other questions remain to be answered but suffice it to say here that the Look East Policy has to be explained to our people on a mission mode because if the people are excluded from this Policy, it has no hope of being successful.

Direct connection with the people then is paramount. How to go about it? In-depth study of the societies, cultures, ethos, belief systems, traditions, etc. is primary as much as in-depth study of the characteristics, psychological profiles and aspirations of the people. Interventions to treat and heal physical, mental and psychological wounds must be worked out. Perhaps we can be guided by the UNDP's Crisis Prevention and Recovery process particularly the first step, which is "understanding of current situation, needs and gaps to assess what already exists, avoid duplication of efforts, and build on existing information and capacities". This is done through a systematic inventory and evaluation of existing risk assessment studies, available data and information, and current institutional framework and capabilities.

If we are truly searching for solutions to the problem, often spelt as India's Northeast, at one level, we have to start right from the time of Independence, if not politically definitely psychologically and economically. But even politically there are many wrong that can still be righted, which would strengthen India's democratic traditions and credibility. Politically, the first move would have to be the scrapping of the Armed Forces (Special) Powers Act, 1958, as well as other similar Acts that not only violate human rights but more importantly damage India's democratic cultures and credibility. The gun cannot resolve majority of the problems and conflicts in the Northeast; more often than not, not even money can. What the Northeast requires is the honest application of the principle of hands-on, sincerely and seriously. We have a Ministry of Development of the NER for the infrastructure and physical development of the region. Now we need a Ministry or some such body for the human security development of the people of the region that must be supervised and monitored by a hand-picked group of dedicated people, composed of experts in their own fields, perhaps akin to the erstwhile Indian Frontier Administrative Agency (IFAA).

Inarguably, because of geographical, geo-political, economic, social and cultural factors, India needs to open up the Northeast to our Eastern neighbours. This has to be clearly enunciated to the people. India should not and cannot afford to depend on Northeastern political classes to do this because they are one of the primary causes of disenchantment, and often aggravators and agent provocateurs of various kinds of conflict, in this region. When the mind is open and willing, a way will always be found. Ultimately, it is a question of how badly we want to address and redress the multi-faceted impact of the varied and various conflicts in Nagaland, indeed in the Northeast.

Impact on Assam, Mizoram, Meghalaya and Tripura

Samir Kar Purkayastha

Stories of conflict have to be told, so that we cherish peace.

Stories of unrest in India's Northeast is perhaps as old as its civilization and so is its quest for peace. The region is home to more than over 200 different ethnic groups and sub-groups that communicate in about 400 different languages and dialects. This ethnic potpourri in itself is a recipe for conflict. Particularly so, as these large ethnic groups had to share limited agricultural land. And so they have to be fiercely protective about their territory. Diversities in terms of ethnic origins and a long history of virtual absence of cultural and economic exchanges among these distinct groups further accentuated ethnic discord and generated cleavages along ethnic conceit. As a result, early history of the region was marred by stories of turf wars, head huntings, raids and inter-tribal warfares.

The British policy of keeping the large sections of these diverse groups isolated through Inner Line Regulation of 1873 and the declaration of most of the hill areas as "Excluded Areas" under the provision of Government of India Act of 1935, did not help improve the situation.

In post-independent India, underdevelopment, corruption, unemployment, influx of outsiders, over and above the region's cultural and ethnic differences gave further rise to a sense of deprivation and identity losses and fuelled discords in terms of tribal-non-tribal; majority-minority; local-outsiders; hills-plains; inter-tribal and intra-tribal. Such binary disputes have pushed the region into a perpetual state of crisis since Independence and gave birth to a myriad of armed separatist movements.

This paper focuses on the present conflict scenario in the Northeastern states of Assam, Mizoram, Meghalaya and Tripura. An attempt has also been made here to explore the possible solutions to the festering crisis.

Assam

Rear view mirror is often the best and most reliable crystal ball. So before looking into the present situation in Assam, I would like to share a personal experience that will give a broad picture of the conflict scenario in the state a decade before, and will help a better understanding of the present situation.

As a political reporter in a Guwahati based regional newspaper, *The Sentinel*, I had gone to Nalbari to cover electioneering on the run-up to the 2001 Assembly elections. The district was traditionally a stronghold of the then ruling party Asom Gana Parishad. But its party district headquarters was completely desolate at 4 in the evening, just a couple of days before the May 10- poll. I was told that the party functionaries had abandoned the post as the ULFA activists were purportedly on prowl. Only a few days back, on May 4, ULFA extremists had stormed AGP's party office in Bogorihatigaon, (then agriculture minister and senior AGP leader Chandramohan Patowary's constituency) at Dharmapur in the district, killing six party workers and injuring an equal number. The incident was preceded by another attack on a party election office in the same district by the outfit on May 3. Three party workers were killed in the attack. Earlier on March 17, three civilians, believed to be AGP sympathisers, were killed by the outfit, again in the same district. On April 28, AGP campaign office in Guwahati, located barely 500 metre from the then Chief Minister Prafulla Kumar Mahanta's heavily fortified official residence, had been attacked. One party worker died and 14 others were hurt.

Similarly, ULFA had also attacked AGP's office at Dibrugarh on May 1, killing one party worker and a policeman. On the same day, BJP's candidate for the Dibrugarh assembly constituency, Jayanta Dutta and two other party workers were killed by the outfit in the upper Assam town. Run up to the 2001elections had also witnessed life attempts by proscribed ULFA on AGP candidate for the Barpeta assembly seat, Kumar Deepak Das and Samata Party candidate for the Rangiya assembly constituency (in Kamrup district), Dipak Kalita.

In the vortex of violence, democracy was under complete siege. Militants appeared almost as powerful as the State as their writ ran from Dibrugarh to Dhubri. Support for the outfit in Nalbari and elsewhere in the state was palpable. Far from being sympathetic to the AGP-BJP alliance for being at the receiving end of the carnage, the people, whom I had interacted in the district, were angry at the Mahanta-led AGP government for allegedly devising a brutal way of confronting ULFA: secret killing. During 1998-2001, several relatives, supporters and sympathisers of the ULFA were systematically killed by the unknown assailants, in what is infamously referred in the state as *gupto hoitya* or secret killings.

For most Assamese, ULFA at worst were misguided youths who merely adopted wrong means to pursue a right cause.

Secret killing was not the only reason that caused the disenchantment over the existing setup. The state was bogged down by growing unemployment, government's inability to pay salaries regularly to its employees and a staggering economy with the gross state domestic product (GSDP), according to a planning commission figure, growing at a trend rate of about 3.3 per cent per annum during the period from 1980-2001. While the growth rate at the all-India level had picked up after the initiation of the economic reform process in 1991, the Assamese economy did not indicate any change in the trend growth rate in the first decade of the post-liberalization period.

The Assam Development Report prepared by the Planning Commission along with the Government of Assam and Indira Gandhi Institute of Development Research in 2002 pointed out that the most striking fact of Assam's economic development was that it was falling behind the rest of the country. In 1950-51, per capita income in Assam was 4 per cent above national average. In 1998-99, it was 41 per cent below the national average.

The moratorium on fresh recruitment for government jobs, following a MoU signed by the AGP-led state government with the BJP-led NDA government at the Centre as an austerity measure, to revive the state's sagging economy, only increased the sense of neglect and marginalisation among the Assamese youth.

If that was not enough, the disillusionment was completed by the complete failure of both the state and the Central governments to address the issue of influx of illegal migrants from Bangladesh despite both AGP and BJP's avowed stand against infiltration and tall talks of detecting and deporting illegal migrants.

Amidst the existing hopelessness, militancy naturally proliferated. Apart from ULFA several other insurgent groups were waging, what they fashionably called, armed struggle in the state. The BLT and the NDFB were active in the Bodo heartland, while the UPDS and the DHD were blazing guns in the twin hill districts of North Cachar (now Dima Hasao) and Karbi Anglong. Besides, several other smaller groups like the Kuki Liberation Army, Hmar People's Convention (Democratic), Kamtapur Liberation Organisation were also posing threat to the state's security. Adding to the concern of the security agencies in the state, for the first time militancy was also taking root among the hitherto docile Adivasis or the Tea Tribes with the formation of Adivasi Cobra Force in July 1996.

According to an annual report of the home ministry, from 1997 to 2001, Assam had witnessed 2605 incidents of violence. Tripura was the only state in the region, with 2701 incidents, that had seen more bloodshed during that period. More than statistics, what had caused real concern was the dominance of the militants and the public support they were getting.

Compared to those despairing periods, Assam is definitely placed in a much better situation today. Its economy is slowly but steadily growing. Militant groups have either inked accords to return to the mainstream or are engaged in peace talks. And more importantly for the law-enforcing agencies there has been a discernible change in public perception towards insurgents.

The average real growth rate of Assam was 2.21 percent during 1994-2002. The same has increased to 5.91 percent during 2002-2012, registering an increase of 167.4 percent over the earlier period. The corresponding all India rate has been 28 percent.

In terms of growth, per capita income has increased by 6.01 per cent and 7.24 percent in 2010-11 and 2011-12 respectively over the previous years, according to Assam's Economic Survey 2011-12.

Assam chief minister Tarun Gogoi, who also holds the finance and home portfolios, in his 2012 budget speech, highlighted the changed scenario: [1]

---

[1] Chief Minister Tarun Gogoi's budget speech on March 12, 2012.

"Assam has witnessed major changes during the past decade. The security scenario has shown significant improvement with a number of insurgent groups coming over ground. There is a general realisation today that violence provides no answers and that only engagement in the democratic process can enable diverse groups to fulfil their aspirations. This feeling has in no small measure resulted from a realisation that the government is working for the people and for their all-round betterment. I am sure that the remaining insurgent groups will understand the sentiments of the people of Assam and come forward to create an atmosphere that is conducive for accelerating the pace of development in Assam.

During the same period there has been a significant improvement in the financial resources of the State. Substantial resources have been generated by enlarging the tax base and improving the tax compliance. The plan size of the State has increased substantially from Rs 1521.28 crores during 2000-01 to Rs 9000 crores during 2011-12. Multi-lateral channels of funding from agencies like ADB, Japan International Cooperation Agency (JICA) and the World Bank have been opened up. With the enhanced resources a number of schemes and programmes for speedy and accelerated development of Assam have been taken up. These are some of the reasons for the phenomenal rise of the GSDP growth rate in Assam, which is expected to exceed 8 per cent during the current year as against the average growth rate of 1.97 per cent during the Ninth Plan Period of 1996-97 to 2001-02."

Apart from those complex statistics, there is also visible sign of development on the ground zero. The state government today is not only able to pay regular salaries to its over 5 lakh employees; it has also implemented the recommendation of the 6th pay panel with effect from February 1, 2010.

The economic recovery has had a cascading impact on the militancy. An Assamese youth today is keener to be a part of the growth chart than charting a future in the wilderness carrying Kalashnikovs or lethal explosives.

There are also other factors that significantly contributed in ebbing militancy in the state. The first and foremost among them was Operation All Clear launched by the Royal Bhutan Army on December 15, 2003 against the Indian militants holed up in the Himalayan Kingdom. ULFA had 13 camps, the NDFB 12 and the KLO had 5, scattered across the dense jungles of the kingdom's southern districts of Samtse, Kalikhala, Sarpang, Nganglam, Samdrup, Jongkhar, Bhangtar and Daifam. The geographical contiguity of the jungles allowed the militants, estimated to be around 1500, lodged there, an easy access to and from Assam, where their depredations continued.

In the offensive, all the 30 camps were razed, including the ULFA's central headquarters at Phuakaptong in Sandrup Jongkhar and its general headquarters at Merengphu in the same district. Among others, ULFA ideologue Bhimkanta Buragohain, its publicity secretary Mithinga Daimary, NDFB publicity secretary B Erkadao and top KLO leaders Tom Adhikary and Milton Burman were arrested during the operation. In all, 650 militants were either killed or apprehended or made to surrender in the offensive.

Though there is a debate over the real success of the operation as most of the top brasses of ULFA and the NDFB managed to escape to Bangladesh ahead of the strike, it undoubtedly considerably depleted the strength of the state's two most powerful militant outfits and completely demoralised the morale of their low-rank cadres. This in-turn has a far-reaching impact in shaping the course of insurgency in the state and alienating the people from the lofty ideologies of the militants.

Growing influence of Bangladesh over these militant groups in the aftermath of the operation has only proved to be counterproductive, particularly for ULFA which was formed out of a movement against the alleged overwhelming presence of illegal Bangladeshis in the state. Assamese people were definitely not impressed to find their boys relying on the country, whose impoverished citizens are alleged to be threatening the demographic profile of the state through illegal immigration. Likes of Assam police's intelligence chief Khagen Sarma were quick to grab the opportunity to unleash a PSYOP against the outfit by indicating that ULFA Chief Paresh Barua has become more Bangladeshi than most Bangladeshis illegally residing in the state. They widely publicised that Barua had been using the name Kamruj Zaman Khan, alias Zaman Bhai, in Bangladesh. His wife Bobby has assumed the name Sufia Begum and the couple's two children are known as Tahshim Khan and Akash Khan.

Besides, drooping morale and diminishing cadre strength also means both ULFA and the NDFB were no longer capable of engaging security forces in direct combat or going for high-risk selective killings. So in desperation to make their presence felt, both the outfits resort to planting bombs, which was relatively safer to execute and far more effective in terms of inflicting casualties and making impact.

Soon after Bhutan operation ULFA carried out a deadly bomb blast in Dhemaji town on August 15, 2004, in which at least sixteen school children were killed and forty others were injured. It followed the bloodbath by setting off a chain of blasts at different places all over Assam on August 25 and 26, 2004, killing seven persons and seriously injuring 90.

From gun blazing guerrillas targeting security forces at secluded highways to invisible terrorists, planting powerful bombs at busy public places, the face of terror in the state has transformed. 2008-serial blast in Guwahati and elsewhere in Assam was the most grotesque demonstration of this latest face of terror, leaving the nation watching it in their living rooms, live on their television screens in shocked stupor. Terror had come home. Violence no longer meant heroism, or combat in faraway battlefields. It was dying when one least expected.

Even the staunchest ULFA sympathisers could no longer feel safe. Its targets were now unarmed-innocent civilians. In Assamese mind space, ULFA soon morphed into terrorists from revolutionaries. As a result, its crack-units on the ground found it extremely difficult to operate and started distancing from the policies of their leaders based in Bangladesh. The outfit's most dreaded 28 Battalion after severing ties with the leadership came overground in June 2008.

India-friendly Awami League's return to power in December 2008 elections in Bangladesh struck a further blow to the Northeastern militants based there. The new government in Dhaka, as expected, was no longer sympathetic to the anti-India activities of these groups. Within a year of its assuming power, Sheikh Hasina government launched a massive crackdown against these groups and flushed them out of her country in December 2009. Pushed to the corner, the ULFA and the NDFB leadership, handed over to India by Bangladesh, had no other option but to talk to the government to hammer out a negotiated settlement to their demands.

Signing of a peace deal by the BLT on February 10, 2003 and ceasefire agreements by the NSCN (IM) in August 1997 and the NSCN (K) in April 2001 too had influenced return of peace in Assam, and for that matter in other parts of Northeast, to a certain extent.

Bodoland Territorial Council Accord signed by the BLT, had automatically put the rival NDFB under pressure to join the mainstream like the BLT as the fruits of development borne by the council were cornered by the ex-tigers and their sympathisers. On the other hand, the smaller groups like the DHD, Cobra militants and HPC (D), who were raised, trained and supported by the Naga militants were affected by the withering of insurgency in Nagaland.

Combination of all these factors today created a situation wherein almost all the militant groups, barring Paresh Barua-led faction of the ULFA, active in the state are either in the process of disbanding after just signing the peace accords or are engaged in peace parleys with the government. In fact, on 8 October 2012, the Centre and the Assam government sealed a peace pact with two factions of the DHD. Last year, the UPDS shunned the path of violence and joined the electoral politics. Ranjan Daimary faction of the NDFB, though is yet to formally join the peace process, its incarcerated chairman is holding back-channel negotiation with the government representatives to prepare ground for a formal peace parley.

The MHA in its annual report 2011-12 observed:

"The security situation in Assam has improved since early 2010 coinciding with falling level of violence orchestrated by insurgent groups. A total of 31 persons, including 14 SF personnel, were killed in 145 incidents of violence perpetrated by United Liberation Front of Assam (ULFA) (anti-talk), National Democratic Front of Bodoland (NDFB) (anti-talk), KPLT and other UGs in the year 2011, as compared to the killing of 65 persons, including 12 SF personnel, in 251 incidents in the previous year."

In fact, the declining trend in violence has been noticed for the past few years. Number of incidents had come down to 387 in 2008 from 474 in 2007. Though it increased to 424 in 2009, it again dropped to 251 in 2010 and 145 last year.

So after enduring insurgency for decades, is Assam finally on the road to lasting peace? Not really. The state's most dreaded insurgent leader Paresh Barua is still at large. He has the capacity to upset the peace table in the state, given the slightest opportunity. Already concerns are expressed at certain quarters that the India's success in Bangladesh had pushed Barua closer to China.

Moreover, ebbing organised militancy does not necessarily mean end of conflicts. The communal clashes in July this year at BTC- administered districts is the grim reminder of this unpleasant truth. The strife had rendered over 4.8 lakh people, mostly Muslims of Bengali origin, homeless. Around 100 lost their lives. Much to the chagrin of the peace makers, it was the former BLT leaders, and not any militant groups, who had shunned violence to become administrators and law-makers were alleged to be one of the confronting parties. Police had even arrested one of the leaders of the Bodoland Peoples Front (BPF)—the new avatar of the BLT—Pradeep Brahma on charges of rioting, looting and criminal conspiracy. Brahma is a sitting MLA of Kokrajhar (West) constituency.

Worst, the genesis of the communal flare up could be traced to the peace accord signed with the BLT. The accord has given political and administrative rights to the Bodos, who account for not more than 30 per cent of the total population. The peace deal thus sowed the seeds of fresh discontentment among the Bengalis, Adivasis and Assaemse communities, residing there from ages.

Mizoram

In the context of Northeast, except for the Mizo Accord – a 1984 peace deal between the rebel Mizo National Front and the Government of India – no pact with any militant group resulted in a lasting solution of the conflict. Even the Mizo Accord, which upgraded Mizoram from a Union Territory to a State, has largely addressed the aspirations of the state's largest Lushai community, leaving smaller tribes within the constructed Mizo ethnicity like the Hmars and the Brus disgruntled. The Hmar insurgency and issue of Bru (Reang) refugees thus continue to blot the state's claim of attaining peace.

Raking the long-pending demand for Hmar autonomy, the main political party representing the community, the Hmar Peoples Convention (HPC), on May 23, 2012 alleged that the Mizoram government had failed to implement the Memorandum of Settlement (MoS) the state government had signed with it (then it was an armed group) on July 27, 1994.[2] The HPC is peeved over the delay in elevating the status of the Sinlung Hills Development Council, formed out of the 1994-peace pact, to a full-fledged Autonomous District Council under the Sixth Schedule of the Indian constitution as was assured during the signing of the accord.

The HPC even went on to accuse the Young Mizo Association, the state's most powerful and largest pressure group of putting a spanner into its ADC demand. The rift between the YMA and the Hmar community took a new dimension when at least 16 YMA units in the proposed ADC areas had resigned on April 25, 2012, adhering to a "dissolution order" served by the militant HPC (D), an offshoot of the HPC, formed following the differences over the 1994-accord.

To co-opt the smaller ethnic groups within the generic Mizo identity, the Lai Autonomous District Council had been formed on April 29, 1972; the Mara Autonomous District Council, on May 29 1971; and the Chakma Autonomous District Council, on April 29, 1972. But the successive Mizo governments after the statehood ironically are not willing to give any such concession to the smaller groups as has been evident from the recent remark of the Mizoram home minister R. Lalzirliana. Rejecting the Hmar's ADC demand, he reiterated, on April 25, 2012, that, "Three ADCs had been created in Mizoram without our consent. As Mizoram was a Union Territory at that time, we could not do anything. We are not giving any more ADC for any tribe." [3]

The problem of rehabilitation of Bru refugees is yet another contentious issue confronting Mizoram today. The fourth phase of repatriation of Bru

[2] http://www.e-pao.net/GP.asp?src=20..240512.may12

[3] Zodin Sangha, *The Seven Sisters Post*, April 26, 2012

refugees from Tripura to Mizoram ended unsuccessfully on May 15, 2012, after a fresh demand for the creation of an autonomous council on their return to Mizoram had been raised.[4] Some 35,000 Bru refugees fled Mizoram and took shelter in six relief camps at Kanchanpur in North Tripura, following ethnic-violence of 1997. The immediate cause of the conflict (between ethnic Mizos and Bru tribesmen) was the demand for an ADC in the Bru-dominated areas of western Mizoram by the Bru National Union, a political organisation of Bru tribesmen formed in 1994.

Surely, unless the bigger community within the Mizo ethnicity does not show more magnanimity to accommodate the aspiration of the smaller tribes, the state could soon find itself back to the days of turmoil negating all the gains of the statehood accord.

Meghalaya

Such ethnic divide has pushed neighbouring Meghalaya, which was the abode of peace even two decades back, into a perpetual state of crisis today. Significantly, insurgency in Meghalaya was actually started against the domination of the 'dkhars', a sneering term, tribals in the state use to refer non-tribals. Initially, all the three dominant tribes of the state — the Khasis, Jaintias and the Garos — were waging a joint movement against the outsiders under the banner of Hynniewtrep Achik Liberation Council (HALC). But soon what was essentially a fight against the outsiders, turned into inter-tribal rivalries leading to a split on tribal line in the HALC in 1992. The Hynniewtrep National Liberation Council (HNLC) and the Achik Matgrik Liberation Army (AMLA) were formed out of the split. AMLA was subsequently replaced by the Achik National Volunteers Council (ANVC)

Now the fight is no longer primarily directed towards outsiders. One tribal group is pitted against another. Though not too long ago these communities were peacefully co-existing and had a common aspiration and cause. The HNLC, representing the Khasis and the Jaintias, started demanding an end to what it called, a Garo dominance in Meghalaya. The argument is that, Garos have produced more chief ministers than the Khasis and the Jaintias. The ANVC on the other hand is for creating a separate

---

[4] *The Assam Tribune*, May 16, 2012

Garo homeland, carving out Garo Hills from the state. It claimed that Garos were neglected. Once the ANVC declared truce with the government in 2004, the Garo National Liberation Army came into being to fill the vacuum.

Meghalaya is among the few Northeastern states that has bugged the trend of improved law and order in recent years largely because of the subversive activities of the GNLA. Even the home ministry in its annual report 2011-12, while rounding up the security scenario in the region, observed that Meghalaya has witnessed an upswing in the insurgency-related incidents.

To reverse the trend major counter-insurgency operations have been launched jointly by the Assam and Meghalaya police with the help of paramilitary forces in recent months against the GNLA. The operation has, however, so far failed to achieve the desired result. The GNLA continues to hold sway over the Garo Hills even after the arrest of its chairman Champion R Sangma in July this year. Sangma was arrested by Bangladesh police from an apartment in Dhaka and handed over to Indian authorities. More than ideologies, militancy in Meghalaya is driven by the lure of huge extortion-money the state's mining sector fetched to their coffer. The militant activity by and large is restricted to extortion and kidnapping for ransom. As such, while seeking solution to the problem, it should be viewed more as a law-and-order problem triggered mainly by underdevelopment and unemployment, rather than a political one.

Tripura

Tripura is another state in the region where insurgency is dormant for the last few years. A sustained and well planned, both overt and covert, counter-insurgency operation coupled with governance and development interventions did the tricks. Both the state police and the military intelligence used "Trojan horse" techniques to attack rebel bases and leaders across the border in Bangladesh.[5] Another significant aspect of the counter-insurgency operation in the state was its record in upholding human rights.

Former Director General of National Human Rights Commission (NHRC) Sankar Sen during a seminar in Agartala in August 2010, stated

---

[5] Subir Bhaumik, *Troubled Periphery: Crisis of India's Northeast.* (Sage Publication; New Delhi, 2009).

that, "the experience of Tripura police in counter insurgency operations and its success in containing insurgency without violating the rights of the common people can be a model in the country....." [6]

Unlike the CI-Ops in rest of the region, where it lead to further alienation of the common people, in Tripura there was no antagonism against it. These, perhaps could be possible largely because of the pivotal role played by the state police that has a better understanding of the local ethos and identify more closely with the local society.

The police action was backed by slew of development and confidence-building measures which the state government had initiated to reconcile the tribals within the existing setup. It ensured that the community is not left out of the development process by strengthening the grass-root institutions like autonomous development councils. The government delivery mechanism in the far-flung tribal dominated areas too was improved by providing land rights and other benefits to the poor tribals. Till July, 2012, more than one lakh tribal families were given land rights under Schedule Tribes and Other Traditional Forest Dwellers (Recognition of Forest Rights) Act, 2006. Setting up of forest villages with all basic facilities since 2003 to settle the scattered tribal families was another sagacious development initiative that helped in dwindling the support base of the insurgents in the state.

The multi-pronged strategies triggered split and surrender of the militants since 2003, severely denting the striking capacities of both National Liberation Front of Tripura (NLFT) and the All Tripura Tiger Force (ATTF), the two potent insurgent outfits of the state. To keep its catch out of jungles, the state government also came up with attractive rehabilitation package for them.

The back-to-back victories of the ruling Left Front in the elections for the Tripura Tribal Areas Autonomous District Council held in 2005 and 2010 were clear indications of tribal allying with a state's mainstream party rather than insurgent backed Indigenous Nationalist Party of Tripura.

---

[6] *The Hindustan Times*, 31 August 2012

However, despite a spell of peace, like in case of Assam, it will be too early to write the epitaph of insurgency in Tripura. Militants are weakened but definitely not weeded out and given an opportunity they can raise their ugly heads once again.

In the words of state Chief Minister Manik Sarkar:

"Militants have become weak and cornered as the people of Tripura have isolated them. But they are not yet uprooted. To say they are totally inactive is not true, even today they are very active, only that compared to earlier days their activities have come down. According to information with us there are still twenty to twenty-two camps of Tripura-based militants in Bangladesh."

Conclusion

From Tripura to Assam, the broad picture that is emerging today is a perceptual change in favour of peace. People, fed up with long spells of violence, are willing to give peace a chance and are mounting pressure on the militants to shun the path of violence and seek a negotiated settlement of their problem. But to assume that as an end of insurgency and conflict and a beginning of an era of peace will be a rather slipshod reading of the situation.

True, under civil-society pressure, several insurgent outfits across the region have started dialogues with the government. Dialogues, however, draw out room for compromises and concessions. Unfortunately, in a heterogeneous region like Northeast, concession granted to reconcile with a specific group or community often leads to alienation of another. For instance, the alienation of a large section of Assamese society was started with the disintegration of Assam to create smaller tribal states to accommodate the aspirations of the tribal communities.

Migration and settlement expansion by different indigenous communities over the centuries have created a demographic pattern wherein it has become extremely difficult to attribute a specific area or a problem exclusively to a particular community.

Faulty demarcation of boundaries and the divisive policies encouraged by political leadership since Independence have made the situation more complex.

Against such backdrop and a past history of innumerable failed accords, the ongoing peace negotiations and the freshly inked accords by themselves do not stretch out hope for a durable peace. More so, as agreements in the past have mostly been scripted merely to neutralise the erstwhile rebels through political power sharing rather than to sincerely resolve the issues that gave birth to their rebellion. As a result even before the inks on these accords are dried, a new outfit is raised to carry on the "rebellion."

Therefore, the process of conflict resolution should not heavily rely on the talks-bound militant leaders, who are often pushy, unreasonable and unaccommodating. Rather, attempt should be made to win over the support of the common people, who only want a decent earning and a dignified living. Do not herd them together in a village ground like animals in the name of counter-insurgency operation. Do not take away their land in the pretext of infrastructure development. Do not swamp them with migrants. Give them a square meal. And they will be too happy to coexist peacefully.

And yes, the purpose of any future agreement should be to address the genuine problems raised by the insurgents, and not merely creating a new political breed of ex-militants.

Conflict in Assam and its Consequences

Jayanta Kumar Ray

Clashes between Bodos and Muslims, starting in the state of Assam around 19 July 2012, eventually engulfed the five districts of Dhubri, Kokrajhar, Chirang, Bongaigaon and Barpeta in the Bodoland Territorial Autonomous Districts (BTAD). At the height of the disturbances, as many as 340 relief camps accommodated 4, 85,921 displaced persons. Nearly 100 persons lost their lives. The intensity of discords could be comprehended from the fact that, even after the lapse of two months, there were 1, 87,052 persons in 206 camps.[1]

In the assessment of some observers, a number of persons were sent back from relief camps in an unnaturally hasty manner. This was not realistic, because as late as 25 August 2012, seven persons were killed amidst continuing clashes.[2]

One has to look at the past in order to understand the roots of recent disturbances in Bodoland. The area, now designated as Assam, was originally known as Kamrup, where Bodos were the original inhabitants. Bodos have been reduced to a minority in their homeland. Non-Bodos outnumber Bodos in the BTAD. Non-Bodos include Indians, Bangladeshis and many others. Indian Census authorities have not bothered to identify them. Bodos think that they are justified in considering the presence of these foreigners as a threat, and therefore, in expelling them. [3]

Hagrama Mohilary, the Chief of the Bodoland Territorial Council (BTC), has warned that he may have to start afresh an agitation for the formation of a separate Bodoland state, if Bangladeshi migrants are not turned away. In his view, at least two lakh Bangladeshi Muslims crossed

---

[1] *The Statesman*, 17 September 2012.

[2] NirendraDev, Interview with Prafulla Kumar Mahata, former Chief Minister of Assam, *The Statesman*, 22 September 2012.

[3] Patricia Mukhim, *The Statesman*, 3 September 2012.

the international border during the last ten years, and reside in the BTAD. He and his political colleagues are not ready to shoulder any responsibility for these foreigners. Therefore, the ethnic crisis cannot be resolved, unless the government seals the border, and stops Bangladeshi infiltration. The BTC chief, however, has affirmed that Bodos have cordial relations with those Bengali-speaking Muslims who have been living in Bodo territory for years, and possess land rights as also voter identity cards. But Bangladeshi Muslims have formed militant organizations, and engaged in an endeavor to set up a separate Muslim land, consisting of fourteen districts, including the BTAD. Mohilary complains that these militants have established the United Minority National Army inside the BTAD.[4]

An impression has grown, quite naturally that these militants and/or their accomplices have taken some measures, in an evidently organized fashion, against non-Muslim northeasterners residing in a number of cities (far away from northeast India) as a reaction to, or revenge against, what Muslims have experienced in the BTAD. This has to be thoroughly denounced, for, Bodos as well as Muslims have suffered from hostilities and taken shelter in the relief camps of Assam. But non-Muslim supporters or sympathizers of Bodos have not bothered to launch any protest or vengeful agitation against Muslims in any part of India. This fact, however unpleasant, has to be stressed candidly, so that the government can plan remedial measures. Otherwise, democracy and religious toleration in India will face a serious danger.

In this context, some disgraceful and disturbing events have to be recounted. Around the middle of August 2012, some Indian cities, especially Bangalore, Hyderabad, Chennai, Mumbai and Pune witnessed a large scale exodus of non-Muslim northeasterners to their home towns and villages. They were students or employees in various sectors, including the information technology sector. They were so fear-struck that they left by overcrowded trains despite the obvious suffering of women and children. It was indeed good news that within a few weeks – from around the first week of September 2012 – these people began to return to their work places. After all, opportunities for study and employment were far greater in the above

---

[4] Rajib Chatterjee, *The Indian Express*, 6 September 2012.

noted cities than in Northeast India. Many of them have been living in cities like Bangalore for years, and their efficiency has received due appreciation from their employers. It must be acknowledged that the government of Karnataka has performed a remarkable role in facilitating the return journey from Northeast India. For example, the Deputy Chief Minister of Karnataka visited Assam, and assured them that his government was already in touch with their employers, and that their pay for the period of absence would not be deducted. Some employers, too, took personal initiatives to relieve the worries of Northeasterners.[5]

This was all a matter for cheer. Nevertheless, what was extremely alarming and unfortunate was how blackmail and threats were used to stir up instability. For instance, SMS and MMS were used on an enormous scale and in a calculated manner to create panic in the minds of northeasterners, especially by spreading a message that, at the end of a specific religious festival (viz. Ramzan), they would face a nemesis. What happened on 12 August 2012, however, was a real proliferator of terror. A dangerous incident took place in the Azad Maidan of Mumbai on that day, and made it inevitable for northeasterners to rush back to their distant homes. The Raza Academy and a few other Muslim organizations, aided by announcements from some mosques and inflammatory writings in a section of Urdu newspapers, arranged a huge assembly of Muslims in the Azad Maidan on 12 August 2012. Police authorities anticipated not more than 2000 people at the Maidan. Actually, the number reached about 50,000. The assembly was mobilized to protest against recent disturbances in Assam. Some speeches delivered at the meeting and morphed pictures of events in Assam circulated in the meeting were extremely provocative. Troubles started when a band of 500-1000 armed Muslims joined the meeting, and attacked policemen, outraging the modesty of police women, snatching police weapons, assaulting journalists and damaging the vehicles of media agencies. The Mumbai police exercised extraordinary patience, and decided to make themselves the major victims of violence at the Azad Maidan. Only two persons lost their lives in the meeting, due to police action, and fifty persons suffered injuries. Subsequently, the Mumbai police did not make large scale retaliatory arrests, and detained only those miscreants among Muslims in

---

[5] Samudra Gupta Kashyap, *The Indian Express*, 2 September 2012.

the assembly, whose pictures clearly appeared in video cameras, and illustrated their participation in violent activities. The civil society, too, played a highly constructive part. As a result, the much dreaded chain reaction of communal violence and counter-violence did not occur.[6]

The basic question is: 'Will the police in future be able, or should they be required, to observe such self-restraint, almost self-flagellation?' In case the abovenoted militants receive patronage from larger international terror networks, will they be incited by such a demonstration of police restraint to stage more serious and explosive disturbances?

This leads us to an exploration of the root cause of recent conflicts in the BTAD. The root cause is illegal Bangladeshi Muslim migration (or infiltration) in Northeast India, especially in Assam. New Delhi and Guwahati have not only failed to plan appropriate measures to cope with this familiar phenomenon, they have not also demonstrated much enthusiasm on this matter. One principal reason behind this is that ruling circles in Assam have used infiltrators as a reliable vote bank. The resultant demographic imbalance can be a threat to India's culture of democracy and religious toleration does not appear to worry ruling circles in Assam (and New Delhi). That is why the Illegal Migrants Determination by Tribunals Act (IMDT Act for short), enacted in 1983, was nothing but a deception. It was drafted in such a way that it would not have any adverse impact upon the above noted vote bank. For instance, the responsibility to prove Indian citizenship was vested not in the illegal migrants but in the police. Consequently, infiltrators could concoct a number of excuses to escape the penal provisions of the IMDT Act. Assam witnessed a mass movement against infiltration from 1979 to 1985. As a result, New Delhi and Assam signed the Assam Accord on 15 August 1985. This Accord, too, was a sort of fraud. For, it took care largely to keep intact the vote bank of infiltrators for Assam's ruling circle. The central government did nothing in accordance with the 1985 accord to arrest infiltration from Bangladesh. Moreover, negotiations leading to the 1985 Accord were not properly conducted. Those Assamese leaders, who carried out the anti-infiltration movement for six years, were certainly associated with these negotiations. But the Union Home Ministry left out of these

---

[6] Patricia Mukhim, *The Statesman*, 27 August 2012. Ram Puniyani, *Frontier*, Kolkata, Vol. 45, No. 10, 16-22 September 2012, pp 5-6.

negotiations such important stakeholders as tribal leaders, Advasis and Indian Muslims. Therefore, the much-advertised Assam Accord of 1985 was foredoomed to failure.[7]

In 2005, the Supreme Court of India rightly declared the 1983 IMDT Act as void. The logical option for the government was to enforce the Foreigners' Act, which was more effective than the IMDT Act, because it placed the onus of proof of Indian citizenship upon illegal migrants themselves. But New Delhi appeared to be infiltrator-friendly. It did not lose much time in issuing rules and regulations on Foreigners' Tribunals, which would enable infiltrators to counteract the efficacy of the Foreigners' Act.[8]

The problem of infiltration acquired great importance in the context of recent violence in the BTAD. The Union Home Ministry circulated some data about the identification of infiltrators by tribunals and their deportation to Bangladesh. Spokesmen of the Assam government, too, published some data. If one assembles these data, one notes that in Assam, presently, 36 tribunals are working, and they have to deal with 3.2 lakh cases. So far, these tribunals have already disposed of 1.4 lakh cases, declared 60,000 migrants as illegal, and deported 2,400 persons to Bangladesh. The Assam government has urged upon the Union Home Ministry to set up an additional number of 64 tribunals. Interestingly, at least 500 persons, suspected to be Bangladeshis, left relief camps, established after clashes in the BTAD, as soon as they became aware that the process of verification of citizenship rights commenced in these camps. There was reasonably definite information that they returned to Bangladesh. In this situation, remarkably, many other persons simply disappeared from relief camps, although they left sufficient indications that they were journeying towards Bangladesh.[9]

---

[7] R.N.Ravi, former Special Director, Intelligence Bureau, Government of India, *The Statesman*, 24 September 2012. NirendraDev, Interview with Prafulla Kumar Mahanta, *The Statesman*, 22 September 2012.

[8] For relevant details, see Lt. Gen. J.R.Mukherjee, "Conflict and Insurgency", in Jayanta Kumar Ray and Rakhee Bhattacharya, eds., *Development Dynamics in North-East India*, Delhi: Anshah, 2008, p. 214. E.N. Rammohan, "The Northeast Insurgencies: Causes and Solutions", in Jayanta Kumar Ray and Rakhee Bhattacharya, eds., *North East India: Administrative Reforms & Economic Development*, New Delhi: HarAnand, 2008, pp. 117-22.

[9] *The Indian Express*, 14 September 2012

In other words, the problem of infiltration from Bangladesh should no longer be downplayed. For, otherwise, the situation will get more and more complex. A proof of this was available on 28 August 2012, when the All Assam Minority Students Union, in collaboration with thirty other likeminded organizations, sponsored a day-long Bandh in a number of places, including Guwahati. This led to violent incidents—even assaults on journalists – on such a scale as to require the imposition of curfew in some localities. The All Assam Minority Students Union went so far as to proclaim a demand for the abolition of the Bodoland Territorial Council.[10] This also underlines the gravity of the situation, and points to the inadequacy of such stopgap measures – as the blocking of facilities for the dispatch of SMS on a massive scale initiated after the ugly incident of 12 August 2012 on the Azad Maidan in Mumbai – in coping with potentially explosive capacities for disruption in the possession of a body like the All Assam Minority Students Union. [11]

One probable reason why Bodos exhibit uninhibited concern about stopping infiltration from Bangladesh is their lack of confidence in the Union and Assam governments. After all, in the 1960s, the legitimate language agitation of the Bodos (an issue incomparably less complex than that of infiltration) was thoroughly mishandled, and subjected to cruel repression. Eventually, the Bodo language earned recognition as a state language of Assam, and school/college books were written in this language – but not before more than a hundred participants were slaughtered in course of the Bodo language movement of 1974.[12]

There can be debates on the exact number of infiltrators from Bangladesh. Census reports, too, may cause controversies. But the natural lack of statistical accuracy must not be an excuse for deemphasizing the menace of infiltration. After all, an elaborate survey conducted by a top-ranking functionary of the Intelligence Bureau, government of India, has revealed an alarming development: large numbers of illegal settlements have grown up in the urban areas of Assam during the last two decades,

---

[10] *The Statesman*, 29 August 2012.and 3 September 2012.

[11] *The Indian Express*, 29 August 2012,

[12] SantoshRana, "Bodoland: The Killing Field", Frontier, 7-13 October 2012, Vol. 45, No.13, p.6.

and at least 25 per cent of the inhabitants have arrived from Bangladesh only recently. [13]

The troubles in the BTAD and their aftermath have conveyed a warning signal: let there be no mistake about it. If, in the immediate future, Union and state governments fail to deport a sufficiently large number of illegal migrants from Bangladesh, and arrest ceaseless infiltration from Bangladesh, the root cause of such troubles, there will be no dearth of national/ international terror networks to utilize these troubles to endanger India's security as also vitiate its rich culture of democracy and religious toleration.[14]

---

[13] *The Statesman,* 24 September 2012:

[14] J.B.Lama and Patricia Mukhim stress the role of Government of India in arresting illegal migration from Bangladesh: see *The Statesman,* 1 October 2012.

Transborder Insurgency and Effects

Major General Arun Roye

Historical Background

Myanmar's political history began in the 5th century when people called the Pyus founded a kingdom above the Irrawaddy delta under strong Indian cultural influence. Later, the Mons ruled the whole of lower Burma until the Burmans, under King Anawratha, arrived from the North in the 11th century. Warfare with the Mons and Thais continued almost up to the beginning of the 19th century when the Burmans came into conflict with the British. Burma was annexed in stages up to 1885 and became a province of British India. Serious rural rebellions broke out in 1931 and 1937, which led to Burma's separation from India and to limited internal self-government.

The Japanese occupation of 1942-45 gave a group of young nationalists, the "30 Comrades", a chance to rise to political prominence. This group formed the pro-independence Anti-Fascist People's Freedom League (AFPFL), under the leadership of Aung San and U Nu. It was this struggle which brought together the warring ethnic groups such as Kachins, Chins and Shans to a common platform unified by their demand for independence. In July 1947, when independence negotiations with the British were well advanced, Aung San was assassinated. U Nu subsequently became the Prime Minister of the Union of Burma when it gained independence on 4 Jan 1948.

The AFPFL won two subsequent elections, and apart from a two year period (1958-60) under a military caretaker government headed by the Army Chief of Staff, Gen Ne Win, Myanmar enjoyed 12 years of democratic government (1948-62). However, this came to an end in March 1962, when Gen Ne Win staged a coup, replacing the government with a military run Revolutionary Council.

In 1974, a new constitution declared Myanmar to be a socialist one party state ruled by the military's Burma Socialist Programme Party (BSPP).

Myanmar remained shut off from the outside world, a policy that resulted in economic stagnation.

In October 1987, as economy deteriorated continuously, student demonstrations were held in the capital, Yangon. Widespread protests began in March 1988, increasingly focused around the leadership of Aung San Suu Kyi, the daughter of the revered independence-era leader, Aung San. In July 1988, Ne Win resigned as Chairman of the BSPP. The period between July and September 1988 witnessed large-scale protests and a crackdown by the military resulting in heavy casualties. On 18 September 1988, the Head of the Army, Gen Saw Maung, announced the establishment of the State Law and Order Restoration Council (SLORC) and imposed martial law.

Burma or Myanmar, as it was renamed in 1989, is undergoing a transition. In the meanwhile, Aung San Suu Kyi had formed her party, National League for Democracy (NLD), and decided to fight for democracy in her country.The NLD contested the 1990 election and secured more than 80 per cent of the votes. The SLORC needed to convene the parliament within 60 days in July1990. But SLORC ignored the existing laws and ignored NLD's repeated call for a meeting to solve the issue. The NLD leaders decided to form a legitimate government in the country. This move of the NLD was brutally suppressed by the SLORC. In 1993, the Junta established a government funded organization called Union Solidarity and Development Organization (USDA). Than Shwe and his supporters used this organization to raise support for the government. In between these political, social and economic developments, SLORC was dissolved and renamed as State Peace and Development Council (SPDC) in 1997 with leadership under Senior General Than Shwe. On its part, the Junta also took some initiatives in order to influence the people about its good spirit for reinstallation of democracy. In 2003, the then Prime Minister of Myanmar, Khin Nyunt designed a seven point road map for Myanmar, which included a referendum, a new constitution and elections for the country). In 2007, the third biggest movement was undertaken by the pro-democratic youth and volunteers since the 8-8-88 uprising, popularly known as the Saffron Revolution of 2007. Soon the monks took over the leadership of this movement until the SPDC destroyed it completely. Though Khin Nyunt was ousted from the government soon, his thoughts gave a new vista to the government of Myanmar to build a support base in the country and abroad. This proposal was adopted to create a flourishing and democratic Myanmar so that both international and domestic pro democracy supporters could be pacified. In 2010, the USDA was renamed as Union Solidarity and Development Party (USDP) and participated in the national elections. The military used to control the entire economy of the country through three organizations: Union of Myanmar Economic Holdings (UMEH), Myanmar Economic Cooperation (MEC) and Myanmar Investment Commission (MIC).The 2010 November elections were sixth on the list of the seven points projected by the government of Myanmar for the transition to democracy.

March 2011 onward, the country is slowly inching towards democracy under the leadership of Thein Sein, the president. Aung San Suu Kyi was released; her party (National League for Democracy) was permitted to contest the by elections held in April 12 2012 and the party performed impressively. Aung San Suu Kyi too has been elected to the parliament.

Geostrategic Importance

Myanmar sits at the crossroads of Asia's great civilisations of India and China and looks out onto the vast Indian Ocean next to Thailand. One of South East Asia's largest and most diverse countries, Myanmar stretches from the sparkling islands of Andaman Seas in the south right up into the Eastern Himalayan mountain ranges. Myanmar's strategic location and its reserves of natural resources have given it an important position in the region. Most of its neighbours such as China, India, Thailand and Singapore have their own trading, commercial and security interests in Myanmar. India and China along with ASEAN, unlike the western countries, have adopted the policy of constructive engagement with the Generals in Myanmar, rather than to charge them for being undemocratic. China, in particular, has been on good terms with the Myanmar government since 1988.

Myanmar extends 2080 km from North to South and shares border with India, Bangladesh, Thailand, Laos and China. Importance of Myanmar lies in the fact that it provides access to India for Southeast Asia and acts as a bridge between SAARC and ASEAN. Myanmar provides facility to

China to enter Bay of Bengal both through land routes and Irrawaddy River, China has shown interest in use of Myanmar's Inland Water Transport facilities. Besides, the renewed Chinese interest in Myanmar is guided by its easy access to the Indian Ocean Region through Myanmar thereby reducing the vulnerability of its energy flow through the Malacca strait. Myanmar also connects India to China via two old land routes:-

(a) Ledo/ Sitwell Axis. It connects Poshan in the Yunan province of China with Ledo in Assam, through Myitkyina.

(b) Imphal – Mandalay – Yunnan.

Ethnic Insurgency

Myanmar's diverse ethnic population is a result of the country's strategic location, shared borders with China in the northeast, India in northwest, Bangladesh on West and Laos and Thailand on east. As a result, settlers, belonging to different ethnicities have migrated to the extremely fertile land around Irrawady River. However, demographic divisiveness in Myanmar was unknown during the pre-British colonial era. It originated with the sponsoring of the British policy of 'divide and rule' which professed demographic distinction between 'Burma Proper' inhabited by the majority Burman community and 'outer Burma' inhabited mainly by the minorities. While 'Burma Proper' was directly administered under British India, the minorities were allowed autonomy which led to a situation wherein at the time of independence the majority Burmans were not well disposed towards the ethnics in the new set up.

About 40 per cent of Myanmar's population (around 55 million) is composed of ethnic minorities often referred to as ethnic nationalities. Officially there are 135 national races though the major ethnic groups are seven in number – the Arakan, Chin, Kachin, Karenni, Karen, Mon and the Shan. The Burman majority ruling the country and holding key positions in all walks of life accounts for 60 per cent of the population. The ethnic groups are located on the peripheral mountainous areas of the country occupying around 60 per cent the land area while the majority Burmans are in the inland plain areas. Ethnic similarities exist among tribes residing on both sides of the Indo-Myanmar border e.g. Kuki – Chin – Mizos, Indian and Myanmar Nagas etc.

Myanmar has been ravaged by a civil war for the last six decades since independence (Jan 1948) between the Myanmar armed forces and the ethnic armed groups.The failure to manage Myanmar's immense diversity has resulted in ethnic conflicts, some of them started even before independence, hence making it the longest civil war in the world. The main demand of the ethnic minorities is greater autonomy and acceptance of their cultural and religious identity in the process of their integration in Myanmar's mainstream.

As the main demand of the ethnic groups for regional autonomy through a federal setup has been denied consistently since independence, by the civil and military regimes, the ethnic groups have been involved in a civil war from that time till date. A temporary peace prevailed in most of the ethnic controlled areas when 17 of the ethnic armed groups entered into ceasefire agreements with the military government between 1989 and 1997.

Gen KhinNyunt, the former intelligence chief and deposed prime minister (who was under house arrest since 2004 and released under an amnesty in Jan 2012) was the main architect for the ceasefire arrangements entered into. Post 2009 and post 2010 elections. Some of the ethnic armies, who had signed the ceasefire agreement with the government in 1994, started rearming themselves after the Myanmar army asked them to assimilate with the country's Border Guard Forces and come directly under junta's rule. This would mean downsizing and reorganizing the ethnic groups along with the army with training, logistics, maintenance and remuneration being the army's responsibility. Except for a few smaller groups, none of the ethnic armies agreed to join the BGF. Once the junta started pressurizing the ethnic groups on the issue with repressive tactics, they started rearming themselves. Those who agreed to join the BGF were permitted to register themselves as a political party and contest the general and state elections. The dissident ethnic armies refused to accept the 2010 elections as legitimate and fighting between the ethnic armies and the junta intensified in the forward areas. The attacks increased with demands of respective separate states becoming louder and louder. The Kachin Independence Organisation, one of the most prominent ethnic armies in the country, led the offensives against the junta in areas bordering China in Kachin state and northern Shan state. It had signed the ceasefire agreement with the government in

1994, but reportedly, started rearming itself ahead of the general elections last year Karen and southern Shan state, bordering Thailand, also saw some strengthened offensives against the junta, which responded by brutally cracking down on the dissidents in the area. The Shan State Army suffered major setbacks by proactive military crackdowns since the beginning of the year. Most of these agreements were unwritten understanding or arrangements and varied in content also from group to group. The major groups that did not enter into any ceasefire agreement were the Shan State Army South, Karenni National Progressive Party and the Karen National Union. Subsequently, in February 2011, 12 major ethnic minorities joined forces to form the United Nationalities Federal Council with the aim of forming a bigger, stronger and combined armed force. Having faced brutal offensive actions by the Myanmar army, the UNFC changed its position in May to constitute six associations, which would have their own political party and armed forces and increase their zone of influence.

The ethnic groups in Myanmar are divided into seven classifications – Tibeto-Burman, Burman and Mon-Khmer, Tai, Karen, and Burman, Mon-Khmer and Burman and Shan. There are six major ethno-linguistic groups – Rakhine/ Arkanese, Chin, Kachin, Karen, Mon and Shan and over a hundred ethnic minorities.

TIBETO-BURMAN

☐ Burman

■ Chin

■ Kachin

■ Rakhine

■ Other

**BURMAN AND
MON-KHMER**

■

TAI

■ Shan

KAREN

■ Pao, Kayan, Karenni

KAREN AND BURMAN

■

MON-KHMER

░ Mon, Wa, Palaung

BURMAN AND SHAN

■

MYANMAR

Ethnic Mosaic

Myanmar, which relaunched peace talks with
ethnic groups that have fought for more
autonomy, is dominated by ethnic Burmans
but has more than a dozen other minorities.

Source: 'Burma: Insurgency and the Politics of Ethnicity' by Martin Smith

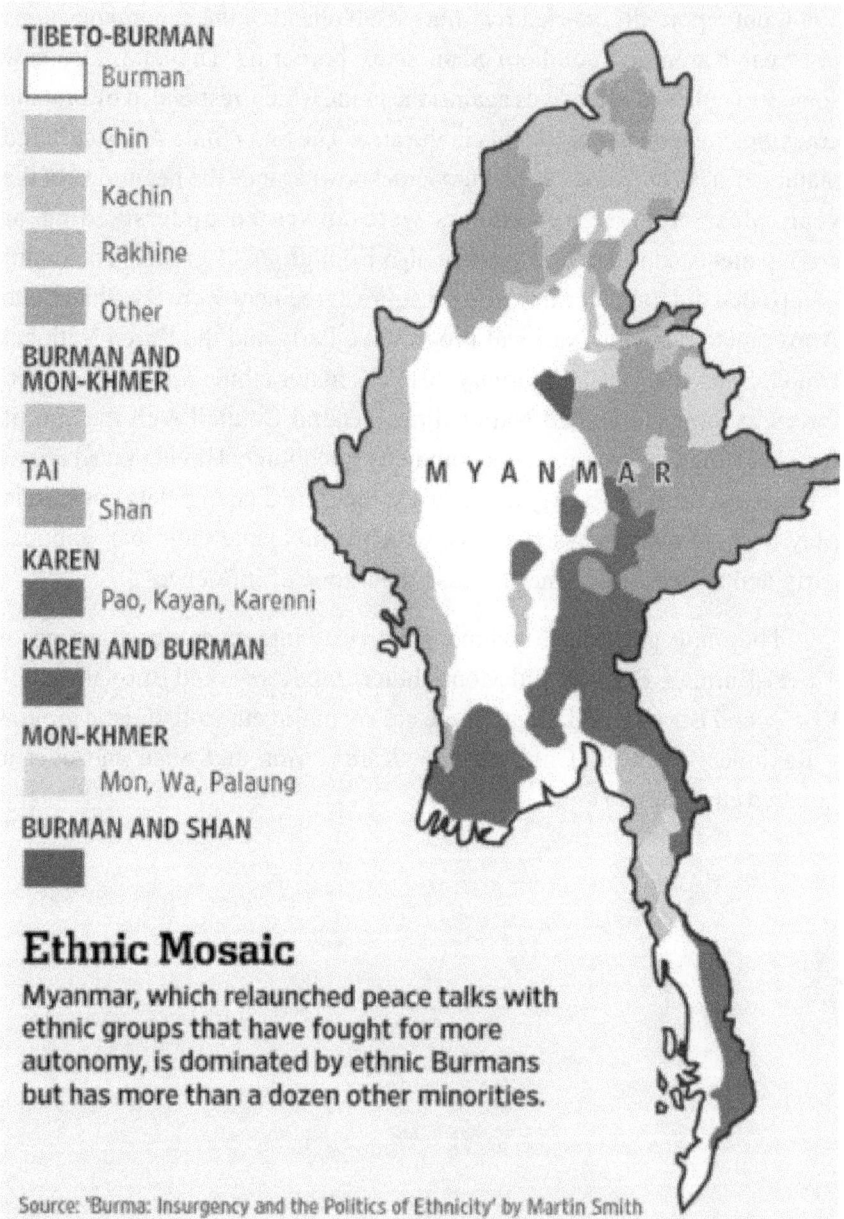

Ethnic Armed Groups

The strength of armed rebels in each group is an estimate and the demarcation
of the areas occupied by these groups is also approximate as they are
frequently changing:-

(a) United Wa State Army (UWSA). – Troops 20,000 to 25,000, the largest ethnic armed group in Myanmar, signed ceasefire agreement in 1989, rejected the Border Guarding Force (BGF) proposal.

(b) Kachin Independence Army (KIA).– Troops10,000, founded in 1961, second largest and considered best organised ethnic group, Kachin Independence Organisation (KIA) is the political wing, one of the parties that signed the Panglong agreement, ceasefire agreement in 1994, has rejected the BGF plan.

(c) Shan State Army (SSA). Troops 6,000 to 10,000, political wing is the Shan State Progressive Party (SSPP). The two factions Shan State Army-South which did not enter into a ceasefire agreement and the Shan State Army-North which entered into a ceasefire agreement in 1989 have been integrated into a combined force since May 2011. Some units of the SSA-N faction have joined the BGF.

(d) National Democratic Alliance Army (NDAA). Troops 1200, also called the Mongla Group. Signed a ceasefire agreement in 1989.

(e) Chin National Army. Troops 500 to 1000, political wing is the Chin National Front

(f) Karen National Liberation Army (KNLA). Troops 2000 to 12,000, political wing is the Karen National Union (KNU), did not enter into any ceasefire agreement.

(g) Myanmar National Democratic Alliance Army (MNDAA). Also known as the Kokang group. This group was attacked in Aug 2009 by the Myanmar Army and the capital Laogai seized. 30,000 residents reportedly fled to China.

(h) Democratic Karen Buddhist Army (DKBA).A group of 6,000 split from the parent organisation KNU in 1994, political wing Democratic Karen Buddhist Organisation (DKBO), first ethnic armed group to join the BGF. Many defections including complete units have been reported since it joined the BGF.

(j) New Mon State Party (NMSP). Troops 700, ceasefire agreement signed in 1995, rejected to be transformed into BGF.

The Government and the Ethnic Groups.

The government after independence went back on its commitment to provide autonomy to these ethnic groups on their joining the Union of Myanmar. The military government that took over in 1962 steadily increased its armed forces with counter insurgency as its main function. The Myanmar Tatmadaw (armed forces) which had strength of around 135,000 in 1964 is today estimated to be 400,000 strong and the second largest military force in South East Asia next to Vietnam's. The combined strength of the armed rebels of all ethnic groups is estimated to be about 45,000.

The counter insurgency strategy of four cuts ie. cutting the four main links for (food, funds, intelligence and recruits) was launched by the Myanmar Government in the 1960s to separate the insurgents from their families and villages. The military resorted to all sorts of repressive measures such as forced relocation of villagers to military controlled areas. Human rights violations such as child labour, looting, rape, use of villagers as porters and grabbing their arable land and produce were often reported but condoned or overlooked by the administration.

Despite these heavy odds the ethnic groups persisted in their struggle as most of them were strategically located in mountainous/ jungle terrain near the borders and in some cases were even supported by the neighbouring countries. The ethnic groups could also subsist by their drug trade and selling timber, jade and other natural resources which were rich in the areas controlled by them. They also resorted to extortion and taxing the locals. However, for some groups it was not just fighting but did develop the areas under their control and introduced welfare measures in health, education and infrastructure. The government finally decided to enter into ceasefire agreements with 17 of the armed groups between 1989 and 1997.

The Ceasefire Agreement

Gen Khin Nuynt, the former intelligence chief and deposed prime minister, is known to be the mastermind for entering into ceasefire agreements with 17 of these ethnic armed groups between 1989 and 1997. Most of these agreements were unwritten understanding or arrangements and vary in content also from group to group. The ethnic armed groups have been allowed to retain their arms and control extensive areas under their control.

The major groups that entered into ceasefire agreements are from Kachin, Kayah (Karenni) Shan, Rahine, Mon, Wa, Pa-o and Palaung. The major groups that did not enter into ceasefire agreement are the Shan State Army-South, Karenni National Progressive Party and the Karen National Union. There are three main reasons for this unusual gesture on the part of the military junta:-

(a) The ceasefire accords have allowed the military to avoid multiple enemy fronts in the aftermath of the 1988 pro-democracy uprising.

(b) Has enabled the Burmese military to make unprecedented advances in its relations with neighbouring countries – especially China and Thailand – in both security and economic terms.

(c) The ceasefire accords gave the military regime the much-needed political legitimacy that they have lost since the bloody crackdown on the 1988 pro-democracy uprising.

Indian Insurgent Groups (IIGs)

Linkages have existed among Myanmar rebels and IIGs for long. It was NSCN (IM) leadership which took the ULFA leaders to the Kachin Independent Organisation (KIO) in eastern Burma, who were having problems with the Burmese government and asked the KIO to help the ULFA by selling them weapons and training in guerrilla warfare. The KIO agreed and a stream of ULFA cadre made their way to Kachin country after a long trek from Kanubari tea estate near Sonari in Upper Assam. The training was hard and brutal and the relatively soft Assamese boys were transformed into hard, tough and battle hardened warriors. The weapons given by the KIO although of inferior quality, as they were primarily seized from the Burmese Army, made the nucleus of ULFA's armoury. ULFA subsequently explored various other avenues including Bangladesh, China and Thailand for weapon procurements in its quest to enhance the outfit's potency.

Similarly, cooperation between the Indian Army and their Myanmar counterpart has also existed at times wherein both forces operated jointly against IIGs. For example, in 1995 the Indian government contacted the Burmese government and both armies staged an ambush across the border in Burma, south of Mizoram. The combined group of the ULFA, the NSCN

(IM) and the PLA was taken by surprise by the ambush and fifty eight cadres belonging to these three groups were killed and as many weapons recovered. The rest of the group scattered into the jungles. Unfortunately at about this time, the Indian government announced an award for Aung San Su Kyi who was under house arrest by the Burmese government. This led to the Burmese military government withdraw their forces and the Indian Army contingent could not pursue the cadres of the insurgent groups who had scattered in the jungles taking advantage of sudden gaps in the deployment.

Presently, Myanmar serves as the refuge for IIGs operating in north east especially post 'Operation All Clear' by Bhutan and crackdown by the Bangladesh government.

(a) Meitei groups that have significant presence in Myanmar are the PLA, UNLF, KYKL and PREPAK.

(b) Kuki groups operating in Manipur are under Suspension of Operations (SoO) agreement with the government of India and the State government of Manipur, Kuki groups are significant in Number but are functioning under the umbrella organisation of KNO and UPF. Kuki groups presently have no camps in Myanmar but have strong affiliation with Myanmar based insurgencies like the Chin National Army. In case of breakdown of SoO, most of the Kuki groups are likely to take shelter in Myanmar.

(c) NSCN (K), NSCN (IM), ULFA (Anti Talk Group) and NDFB (Anti Talk Group) too operate from Myanmar.

Impact of Myanmar Rebel Groups on Indo-Myanmar Relations

Ethnic similarities, thickly forested border areas and the porous Indo – Myanmar border has added in spilling over of insurgency across the international border. The rebel groups operating from Myanmar soil impact adversely the Indo – Myanmar relation as enumerated below:-

(a) Stable and peaceful periphery is essential for India's unhindered economic progress. Instability & turmoil in Myanmar may lead to a civil war with numerous ethnic & tribal groups waging war with the Myanmar Army.

(b) Mutual mistrust is fostered between both countries as either suspects the other to harbour insurgents who are inimical to its own interests.

(c) The Myanmar rebel groups at some point or other may be used by China against India thereby vitiating the environment and bringing instability in the region.

(d) Availability of safe havens to insurgents and sub optimal response on shared intelligence is a potential irritant between India and Myanmar.

(e) Insurgents of the region, in order to maintain their movement, get indulged in drug trafficking and gun running businesses. The proximity of the region to "Golden Triangle" lends itself for easy access to narcotics and the arms bazaar of South East Asia and offers access to weapons/ammunitions easily. This further complicates the security matrix as more criminal elements get added to the canvass.

(f) Insurgency and terrorism in Myanmar has cascading effect in India's North East and vice versa and by corollary the cost of getting situation under control gets multiplied for both countries.

(g) Extortion by rebels in the border areas inhibit private entrepreneurship as well as siphoning off funds allocated for govt projects besides imposing inordinate delays on completion of the projects.Thus setting a vicious cycle of insurgency, lack of development and poor governance.

(h) Insurgency in the area has adversely affected developmental projects thus impacting surface connectivity which otherwise are prerequisites for promoting border trade and movement of people across the border thus keeping prosperity elusive from the region.

(j) Effectiveness of counter insurgency operations by either country gets diluted as the groups under pressure from one country move their cadres across the border.

Way Ahead

Relations between India and Myanmar have started warming up in the recent times which are evident from mutual visits of high dignitaries from both countries. The historic visit to Myanmar by an Indian Prime Minister after 25 years has heralded a new era in Indo –Myanmar relations. It has signalled the end of India's tight rope walk between its avowed commitment for democracy on the one hand and practising *realpolitik* to match China's engagement with the ruling junta on the other. Both India as well as Myanmar share common security concerns along their borders. Indo – Myanmar relations present plenty of potential for the benefit of both nations and it is imperative that India seizes the moment and the opportunity.

Building trust and sympathetic understanding of each other's sensitivities are keys to harness the vast potential between India and Myanmar at different levels ranging from national to tactical level. However, to curb the insurgency in the region following are recommended:-

(a) A comprehensive and well calibrated policy to deal with this menace be evolved mutually between India and Myanmar.

(b) Military to military cooperation be enhanced. India could offer training as well as military hardware to the Myanmar Army to enhance the latter's efficacy in dealing with insurgents.

(c) Joint or coordinated operations be undertaken by both thearmies.

(d) Effective intelligence sharing mechanism be made functional and effective.

(e) Border Haats and local trade be promoted in the area.

(f) Developmental projects including be those related to improve connectivity be completed in a time bound manner.

(g) Governance be improved and delivery of basic services such as education, health care etc be ensured.

(h) Skill development programmes be undertaken and employment opportunities be created for the local youth.

Impact on Nepal, Bhutan and its Offsets in Sikkim

P D Rai

At the outset I present myself as a representative of the people of the region. I am truly concerned about the security as well as the eco-system for sustainable development. I am a mountain man and hence the special mentions of mountain eco-systems are central to my theme.

Please therefore view my thoughts presented here in that light.

Some of my views are traditional but nuanced. As more churn takes place in our societies, thanks to a variety of growth engines, not the least of globalization and major interconnectivity, I will try and give some more insight. Most of these have come ground up.

Today young people are getting impatient. If you ask me what is it that affects me the most as a people's representative, I will have no hesitation in stating that it is young people's increased and changing aspirations. All around the country, as much as it is in our part of the nation.

The Northeast sends a significant number of students to other parts of the country to obtain 'better' education. Indeed also to find work. Estimates, more like guestimates, place funds transferred out of the Northeast to other cities like Bangalore, Pune, Hyderabad etc. at over Rs. 800 Crores annually. Juxtapose this with the recent happenings when we had the greatest of internal movements of young people in the history of modern India who work in Bangalore and other places, having to leave everything because of racially induced fear.

These are the real challenges but they also represent greatest of opportunity. We need to view it in this light.

I will talk about external impacts on Nepal and Bhutan with offsets in Sikkim. The preamble was necessary to position the context.

If one looks at the map of the region it is fairly clear that Arunachal Pradesh, Bhutan and Sikkim are the quieter parts of the region. Other than the flushing out of militants in 2003 from Bhutan aided by India there is no recorded occurrence of any internal problems. The aim would be to keep it that way. Yes, the issues with China on the boundary dispute continue to occur in the Arunachal border, Bhutan and other parts of Western India. That is historical and everyone here would know it. But about Sikkim's border there is little contention. Apart from a small skirmish in 1967 there is nothing big to report. In fact the Border Trade at Nathula that was re-started on 6 July 2006 after 44 years is still continuing. This was thanks to the 'normalizing' of relations. It is also an indicator of a new normal.

Can we improve on this? Can we build people to people contact at Nathula? We need to figure out a way to do a 'Wagah' border here. Push for it. That is a way to create the new normal in terms of relations with the Chinese. For that to happen perhaps the security perception needs to change a bit in New Delhi.

Sikkim also keeps Bhutan and Nepal separated. Historically Sikkim has been the happy hunting ground for incursions from both Nepal and Bhutan, occupying large tracts of land. The British found it useful to take it over and make it the launching pad for their operations in Tibet which they did successfully in 1903-05 with the Young Husband expedition.

Sikkim's geographical competitive advantage continues as the best mountain passes to the Chumbi Valley and into Tibet are from Nathula (14,200 ft) and Jelepla (13,900 ft). Nathula is just 54kms east of Gangtok, the capital of Sikkim.

I am not dwelling on the development and economic benefits of opening up of trade and people to people contacts. I think we need more such like disruptions to help us normalize our relations. Otherwise the old patterns of dialogue with the Chinese will keep us at the status quo. Remember that Prime Minister Vajpayee changed the positioning and structural frame which led to the Nathula Trade happening. It is time to build on that.

As we move East, we come to a more volatile scenario. Nepal is undergoing political churning with the main issue of 'ethnically (also language) based federalism' as its root issue. Traditionalists (including Royalty supporters) want to continue Centrist philosophy. Prachanda is for the former, since his political survival is based on ethnic federalism.

India may have to recognize this reality. It will need to push for a broader dialogue with leaders of the federal units. We need to remind ourselves that much of what has happened in State making in India is based on this premise. Hence for India it is a tried and tested way.

Moreover, Western NGOs and powers have realized this earlier and have been pushing for this.

Contrary to this, China will back the Centrist way, something that they are familiar with. They do not want to be talking to different power centers. This has been made abundantly clear by the Chinese to the leaders of Nepal.

It is important to note that Nepal settled its borders with China in 1960. The reason for Nepal to be friendlier with India has been because of people and cultural ties. Another major factor has been 'access' – to produce and markets. However, the anti-India feeling has always been used to raise the 'nationalistic' sentiments of the people there. Somehow we have not been able to handle this leading to increased 'trust deficit'. The soft power that we have and the advantages that are there for all to see has been wasted.

Now with the frenetic development of infrastructure like road and rail in Tibet to the borders of Nepal will no doubt blunt our 'access' comparative advantage. This will further weaken our leverage with Nepal.

We need to review our 'diplomatic' idioms in this light as much as in light of what has been aforesaid about the 'ethnic federalism' issue.

That brings me to Gorkha Territorial Administration (GTA) and its import. Jaswant Singh, MP Lok Sabha, has stated the following in Parliament:

"Darjeeling is the only district in the country which adjoins four international boundaries. It is the only district which has four nations touching it. If you do not address this as a serious issue of national security, you are doing a very grave wrong to the nation's security and to the citizens of Darjeeling. It adjoins Bhutan, it adjoins Nepal, it adjoins Bangladesh and it is barely 12 kms from the People's Republic of China. It is the gateway to the entire North-East. It is the guardian of the chicken's neck."

As we trace our steps from Arunachal Pradesh to Nepal we find that the vulnerability is at the Chicken's Neck. The idea, therefore, of a stable and secure GTA is one of greatest importance.

Hence in summary let me emphasize the following:

1. That most of all the border State of Sikkim which has become of the foremost states in the country in terms of advancement economically, politically and socially. We have one of the highest human development indices in the country. One of the outcomes has been political stability and peace. Export of ideas for mountain village and eco-tourism to the Northeast is an ongoing phenomenon as much as the ideas of transforming our mountain villages through panchayati raj and local governance. These need to be maintained so that lasting peace is possible.

2. Similarly GTA has to be helped to find enduring peace through development. This is of paramount importance as it affects the State of Sikkim in a number of ways, including politically.

3. Buddhism is the soft power of the area and indeed Sikkim. One of the major contentions in the horizon is the not allowing of Ugen Trinley Dorjee, the 17th Karmapa to take his rightful place at Rumtek. This in time to come will become a huge issue and may affect our prospects of peace in Sikkim.

4. Soft power, through the people of 'Nepali ethnicity' may be used as a cultural and people's bridge to bolster the diplomatic efforts to 'wean' Nepal away from the Chinese cultural and economic influences. Central to this will be the addressal of the growing 'trust deficit'. A long term program can be formulated at the earliest.

5. In Bhutan our efforts need to continue to help them become a more vibrant democracy. I always worry that we may tend to take them for granted.

6. It is important to note here that all the areas that I have dwelt at considerable length are mountain States and Countries. Hence, development paradigms are to be developed in light of the research done for mountain areas. Sustainable development is the key. Institutions like the International Centre for Integrated Mountain Development (ICIMOD) and others in India like the Indian Mountain Initiative will figure significantly in the future.

Finally, our target has to be young people and how we help them achieve their true potential. This is the key. We need to factor this in our development efforts. We have to look at both development and creating sustainable livelihoods for young people as objectives in the short and medium term.

Insurgency in the Northeast-Can this Night without End Ever End?

Major General Sheru Thapliyal

Introduction

Northeast India covers an area of 2, 55,083 Sq. Kms. It shares 98 per cent of its boundary with four countries. It is connected to the rest of India by 28 Km. long Siliguri Corridor. It comprises of 7 states which possess a distinct culture, historical traditions and are in different stages of development in political and economic fields. Physiographically the Northeast comprises of three distinct regions – Assam Valley, Purvanchal Region which includes Nagaland, Tripura, Mizo Hills and Cachar hills and Meghalaya & Mikir Region. The complete area is inhabited by 213 different tribes speaking 325 different languages.

In an insurgency area the space is occupied by five actors. These are the society, the insurgents, the administration, the politicians and the security forces. The key to success is to increase the space of the society and reduce that of the insurgent. The six decade old insurgency in the Northeast continues to endure perhaps because we have not been able to manage this. Much of what ails the region is the result of a feeling of alienation. The term Northeast is not only a physical identity that has been artificially fashioned but also the one that drives New Delhi's political economic and security policies for the region. The policies that New Delhi has been adopting for resolving the insurgency in the Northeast is a mix of military power, suspension of operations, dialogue and cease fire. The Government must realize that all insurgencies in the Northeast cannot be treated similarly and cannot have a similar solution.

An overview of insurgency in the Northeast

When the Constitution was framed, a Subcommittee headed by Gopinath Borodoloi was appointed to examine and recommend the constitutional arrangements that would fulfill the aspirations of the tribal population of the Northeast, and thus set at rest the fears about the possible loss of their unique identity the recommendations of the Bordoloi Subcommittee were extensively debated and incorporated with some amendments into the Constitution as the Sixth Schedule. The Sixth Schedule protected not only the tribal laws, customs and land rights, but also gave sufficient autonomy to the tribes to administer themselves with minimum outside interference. However, as events unfolded, hopes were belied. Tribal insurgencies erupted in Nagaland, Mizoram, Manipur, Assam and Tripura at different points in time. The Mizo insurgency was resolved through a political settlement. The Naga insurgency, the oldest in the Northeast, has been in a state of suspended animation for more than a decade through various ceasefires negotiated from time to time since 1997; but a solution is yet to be found.

The situation in Manipur is probably the worst. The state presents a rather complex picture of ethnic divisions. The Nagas of Manipur hills who feel closer to their kin of Naga hills (in Nagaland) want to be part of Greater Nagaland. Meities, who constitute over 60 per cent of the total population of Manipur want to maintain its integrity, but their demands are secessionist in nature. They maintain that Manipur was never part of India and still is not. The ongoing conflict between the Nagas and Kukis further complicates the situation. The level of violence is quite high. The gravity of the situation may be gauged from the fact that recently a Joint Action Committee constituted by the State recommended that civilians be permitted to possess arms to defend themselves against insurgents.

Tripura, inspite of the 1988 Accord with the Tripura National Volunteer Force, is also faced with a low level of insurgency and keeps regressing into ethnic violence from time to time. The State is surrounded by Bangladesh from all sides, except for a small stretch of the Border which it shares with Mizoram and Assam. Due to a large influx of illegal immigrants since 1947, the local tribals in the State have been reduced to a minority. The resultant clash of interests between the tribals and the immigrants is the root cause of insurgency in the State. The most worrisome aspect of the insurgency is the process of ethnic cleansing undertaken by the likes of the indigenous People's Front of Tripura who have been targeting Bengalis and forcing them to flee the State.

The discontent is Assam has a long history. The 1947 partition of the country started a process by which Assam continued to shrink in size to what it is today. It also resulted in an increased flow of migrants from erstwhile East Pakistan and from other parts of India. Re-organization of the rest of the country on linguistic basis also had its effects on the aspirations of the people of Assam.

The origin of insurgency in Assam can be traced to the Assam Movement started by the All Assam Gana Sangram Parishad (AAGSP) along with the All Assam student Union (AASU) in 1979. It was an agitation against so called "foreigners" and the demographic changes that had occurred due to large influx of migrants. The Assam Accord of August 1985 which brought AASU into power did not bring peace to the state. Encouraged by the success of the violent means adopted by AASU, another militant organization – United Liberation Front of Assam (ULFA) started the agitation for "Swadhin Asom" (Independent Assam).

The ULFA insurgency is still active and has also spread to parts of Arunachal Pradesh. The Bodo area is slowly becoming a flashpoint again, Bodo People's Progressive Front (now running the Bodo Territorial Autonomous District Council) is in conflict with the secessionist National Democratic Front of Bodoland, which is observing a truce with the Centre since 2005. The 2003 Bodo Accord has not been able to restore peace in the region. Further, illegal migration from Bangladesh threatens to change the demographic profile of Assam (and West Bengal) which has serious political and security implications for India. Bangladesh, however, refuses to accept that any of its nationals are staying outside its boundaries and is also opposed to fencing the Assam – Bangladesh border. The situation is further compounded by the external linkages of various insurgent groups operating in the Northeast with Myanmar and Bangladesh. There are reports to suggest that terrorist groups located in Bangladesh are acting in concert with the Inter Services Intelligence (ISI) of Pakistan for spreading terrorism in India.

The Routine Government Response

The situation in the Northeast has been quite delicate since Independence. The Sixth Schedule of the Constitution was a major step to address the problems that were foreseen at that point of time. However, since then there has been no coherent strategy to integrate the region into the national mainstream. The Armed Forces (Special Powers) Act, 1958 (AFSPA) was enacted in 1958, essentially to tackle the situation in Nagaland prevailing at that time and was initially supposed to have remained in operation for one year. The Act continues to be in force and extends to all the seven states in the Northeast. Following large scale protests in Manipur in 2004, a Review Committee was formed by the Government. No final decision has been taken so far and Act continues to be in force.

Every time there has been an agitation or a movement, the response was to deploy the Security Forces, mainly the Army, to conduct counter insurgency operations, followed by a protracted dialogue and announcement of large financial packages for development. In the absence of effective governance in these states, the funds have often found their way to the insurgent groups, the insurgents have given up their ideologies and are indulging in large scale extortions. The victims are the transporters, the traders, government employees, public and private enterprises, and the common man; none is spared. Their aim is to gain power and to control the parallel economy. Insurgency has become an industry and a way of life. In some cases, insurgents have also enjoyed political patronage.

The only insurgency that has been successfully resolved has been that of Mizoram. The two decade old insurgency (1966-86) came to an end with the signing of the Peace Treaty on 30 June, 1986. It is perhaps time to re-visit this success story to draw some lessons which can be applied elsewhere, albeit with modifications.

Recently, a document called 'Northeast Vision 2020' prepared at the behest of the Central Government was released by the Prime Minister. Hopefully it signifies a new beginning for the troubled region but much would depend on its translation into action.

New Delhi recognizes and governs the Northeast, despite its non-homogenous character, only as a fused identity. Consequently, the term "Northeast" is not only a physical identity that has been artificially fashioned, but also one that drives New Delhi's political, economic and security policies for the region. But, the diversity that make up the Northeast are apparent: a Nocte of Arunachal Pradesh has as much in common with a Mising of

Assam, as would a Kashmiri Pundit with a Namboodiri from Kerala, despite the fact that – in ordinary comprehension – both a Nocte and Mising are tribals, just as, in the case of the comparison that is being made, the Kashmiri and Keralite belong to the Brahmin affiliation. It is such indistinct notations that have provided the region with a sense of false homogeneity and – as aforesaid – the character of a "security zone," the latter perhaps as a result of New Delhi's policy towards the encircling nations, propelled, to a significant degree, by circumspection, and the need, therefore, to create a buffer region.

The Reasons for Insurgency in the Northeast

After partition the Northeastern Areas (Reorganization) Act, 1971 created three states Manipur, Tripura ad Meghalaya and two Union Territories, Mizoram and Arunachal Pradesh effective from 21 January, 1972. The two Union Territories became states in 1987. All the states in the Northeast are in the grip of insurgency or have been through insurgency in the past. The reasons for these are near similar and have been enumerated below:-

(a) The roots of insurgency in the area go back to pre-Independence days. The tribes were not brought under a strict political control and rigid regulations. The British tribal policy and Christian education is believed to have queered the pitch for Independent India.

(b) Setting up of reserved forests by British led to the loss of tribal control over natural resources.

(c) Migration of people from the plains and posing economic, cultural and political threat to the tribals.

(d) Lack of good governance, including transparency in its working.

(e) Faulty nation building strategies (economic deprivation)

(f) Inappropriate development.

(g) Large scale unemployment.

(h) Hostile neighbours extending moral and material support.

(i) Lack of good leadership and popular support.

(j) Not anti – India but anti-establishment.

(k) Money for development never reached the target but was diverted to insurgents by politicians to buy security. There was no shortage of recruits as unemployed educated youths joining them.

The Gateway paradigm – A Necessity to end the Insurgency

And so we have, over the past years – with increasing enthusiasm since the early 1990s – the propagation of a new variant of the 'development solution':

(a) South East Asia begins in Northeast India.

(b) For India's Northeast, the future lies in emotional and political integration with the rest of India and economic integration with the rest of Asia.

(c) India's Look East Policy is meaningless, if it does not have an impact on the (Northeast) region.

The logic derives exclusively from location and history, with almost no consideration of current imperatives of geopolitics, capacities, governance and security. As one commentator notes, "The economic approach to the problems of the Northeast seems to be based more on historical romanticism than cold economic facts". In brief, the argument is:

(a) The Northeast is land-locked and has been further isolated by partition and the existence of a hostile Bangladesh, which blocks access to the Indian mainland, except by a tenuous and uneconomical transportation link through the chicken's neck or the Siliguri Corridor.

(b) The Northeast is the 'hub' or ''trijunction' of three great civilisations – the Indian, Chinese and Southeast Asian – with a rich history of cultural and trade relations.

(c) Historically, this trijunction was at the hub of the famed Silk route that enriched the enveloping region, including the Northeast. The locational advantages that fuelled the Silk route still exist, and have been infinitely advanced as a result of the new globalization of the economy and the revolution in transport and communications.

(d) The region is also joined by, and exists as a natural geographical part of multiplicity of regional economic groupings including:

(i) The South Asia Growth Quadrangle (Nepal, Bhutan, Bangladesh and Eastern / Northeastern India)

(ii) SAARC.

(iii) ASEAN.

(iv) BIMSTEC (Bangladesh, India, Myanmar, Sri Lanka and Thailand in an incipient Bay of Bengal Community).

(v) Greater Mekong Sub-region (GMS) – including Myanmar, the Lower Mekong countries of ASEAN, the new China-Yunnan, Myanmar, Laos, Thailand upper-Mekong quadrangle, and the New Mekong-Ganga cooperation project.

(vi) The encompassing Indian Ocean Rim Association for Regional Cooperation (IOA-ARC) and the trans-Himalayan and pan-Asian links being forged by highway, rail and pipeline connections.

(e) By 'opening up' Eastwards, the Northeast would not only secure "wider market access to some of the fastest growing South east Asian and East Asian economies" but this market integration would also create greater trade between India and these countries, with the Northeast "serving as a gateway". This trade would then serve as "a driver of rapid economic development of the region".

(f) 'Export led growth' has been the 'centerpiece of industrial policy' in many countries of Asia, resulting in tremendous development in many countries. This is a model that can be replicated in the Northeast.

(g) Frontier development in the heartland of continents through the development of commercial nodes in border zones along road, rail or inland water corridors creates the potential for the region to become gateways or entrepots.

(h) "The 'Look East Policy' envisages the Northeastern region not as the periphery of India, but as the centre of a thriving and integrated economic space linking two dynamic regions with a network of highways, railways, pipelines, transmission lines, crisscrossing the region".

(i) The Northeast, in addition to its tremendous locational centrality, has immense resource endowments – particularly in bio-diversity, hydro-potential, oil and gas, coal, limestone and forest wealth, and is ideally suited to produce and process a whole range of plantation crops, spices, fruits, vegetable, flowers and herbs.

A great deal of this rhetoric is well intentioned; in other cases, it is simply facile, glib political postures entirely lacking any connect with the realities of the ground. In all cases, however, it reflects either a purely 'macroeconomic' orientation, with a deliberate neglect of the peculiarities of the political economy of the region, or a deceptive superficiality, again with no reference to the situation on the ground. It is crucial to understand:-

(a) You cannot simply order the various components of this supposed strategy off an *a la carte* menu. Take the idea of the separation of 'emotional and political integration' with India, and 'economic integration' with South East Asia. In this fractious region, given the patterns of underlying kinship across national borders and the interests of external powers – including both great and lesser powers in the immediate neighbourhood – how precisely is this to be secured in any but an ideal world?

(b) Various components of the 'paradigm' that has been widely articulated and enthusiastically seized upon need to be evaluated within the realities of the prevailing situation, before large amounts of money and political capital are pumped into another doomed project.

(c) Specifically and immediately, certain unanswered questions arise out of the present concepts of the 'bridgehead' or 'entrepot' paradigm, and these need to be objectively evaluated.

   i. Market integration can lead to both trade creation – through the emergence of new industries; and trade destruction – as a result of the demise of inefficient operation due to exposure to more efficient competitors from integrating countries, and advantages of scale economies that may already exist in these.

ii. The economic transformations that are catalysed by 'integration' may, in fact, bypass the entire traditional sector and replicate the development of 'colonial' sectors, such as tea and oil, which have had a long existence in the region – particularly Assam – with little linkage with domestic local commodity, fact or and money markets, few forward and backward linkages to the larger local economy, and little impact as a driver of growth and general prosperity.

iii. India's relations with neighbouring countries are riddled with political and diplomatic minefields. Bangladesh has had a long history of overt and covert hostility. Border disputes and the memory of 1962 place China in the realm of perpetual suspicion. While India's relations with Myanmar are friendly, but China's overwhelming presence in Myanmar will, again, create potential difficulties and areas of suspicion. China's aggressive expansion across South East Asia and in the Indian neighbourhood is also perceived as a significant threat – both in economic and security terms. Given existing political relationships in the neighbourhood, the actual realization of trade potential is constrained.

iv. Most significant, however, is the fact that little of the existing (formal and informal) trade with the Northeast's neighbours comprised of manufactured goods of local origin. While bicycle exports to Bangladesh were thriving, the only bicycle factory in the region, at Guwahati, was shut down, and export requirements were met from elsewhere despite high transport costs. Existing trade, though substantial in local terms, has resulted in nothing more than the emergence of a few trading centres near the borders.

v. The capital cost of 'integration' and realization of the Northeast's potential does not appear to have been realistically factored into the benign projections currently in favour. A few examples are:-

(a) Rs.228,000 crore at 2002-03 prices for full development of Hydropower potential.

(b) The Stillwell Road project is now conceptualized as part of the Trans Asia Express Way and the Trans Asian Railway that could link Southwest Chinese trading centres and the entire South East Asian region. India's trade with China would then need to cover less than 2000 kilometres, as against the current 6000 kilometre trip through the Straits of Malacca. Cost implication would be staggering.

(c) Rs.93619 crores at 1996-97 prices, for infrastructure development within India. (High Level Commission to the Prime Minister on Tackling Backlogs in Basic Minimum Services and Infrastructure).

(d) Current sea transport accounts for as little as 5 percent of the landed cost of any commodity – consequently, geographical proximity has little to do with trade, except in limited border trade. It is not clear that the massive investments required for developing the Trans-Asian Road and Rail Links will be forthcoming in any rational economic policy framework, as against 'historical romanticism'.

(vi) Resource endowment and location themselves are not enough to unleash a dynamic process of economic development or productive integration. The 'potential' of the Northeast has always existed – but it has not been realized, and there are overwhelming reasons in the political economy of the region why this is the case.

Politico – Military Synergy – Necessary Steps

In any society, especially which is in turmoil, the 'Centre of Gravity' are the people. The focus, therefore, must be on them. It is their perceptions, aspirations, sense of isolation, deprivation, alienation or grievances that need to be addressed. Regrettably, while seeking solutions to these complex problems we tend to ignore them and only consider issues put forth by the insurgents. To be able to achieve resolution of the problem, the state has to function in a transparent, non partisan and credible manner. To that extent, a rejuvenated, conscientious, dedicated and competent bureaucracy has to be in place to ensure effective administration, which is unfortunately lacking in most of the states in the region, due to a variety of reasons.

The problem in Northeast is complex and has various dimensions – ethnic, cultural socio-economic and security. It is thus axiomatic that the solution cannot be found by one particular ministry at the Centre. The Development of the Northeast Region (DONER) ministry is constituted for and focused on development in the Northeast region; development does address some of the aspects stated above, but does not deal with security issues. The Ministry of Home Affairs (MHA) deals with security matters and forces deployed for CI operations in Assam, Nagaland, Manipur ALP and Tripura. There is thus a definite disconnect in perceptions and comprehension of the situation at the Centre between the 'decision makers' (MHA) and the executors (Army formations deployed in various states). The Army HQ functions through the MOD, however, the latter is only on 'listening watch' as 'internal security' is the preserve of the MHA! The harsh truth is that there is hardly any 'Politico-Military Synergy' at the Centre. Consequently, a similar lacuna exists at the state levels, where the Army is considered to be as on "Aid to Civil Authority" format and not in the loop as part of the 'Decision Making Process'. If virtual synergy is to be achieved, there has to be a change in the mind set of the 'Politico Bureaucratic' hierarchy, to allow Army to be a part of the organization. This can only happen if the political leadership asserts itself and interacts with senior military officers directly sans the bureaucrat. To ensure implementation, this change must be effected at the Centre and only then will it percolate downwards. Till this systemic change is brought about, whatever synergy is being achieved at the Centre or the states is purely 'personality oriented' and contingent upon the 'personal vibes' that prevail between heads of various organizations – certainly not the best way to achieve synergy.

It is an accepted fact that there is no military solution to an insurgency, but the military is an essential ingredient of the effort seeking a solution. Political consolidation must follow success achieved by conduct of military operations against the insurgents. It thus emerges that politico – military synergy is the sine qua non for a solution. Some aspects wherein synergy is mandatory to ensure that the CI efforts shall succeed are covered in succeeding paragraphs.

Setting Up of an Expert Security Group at the Centre

Our country like most other democracies is slow to react to a developing internal threat. Weak resolve, political pressures, bureaucratic hurdles and the lack of inter-agency integration and cooperation prevent the formulation of a clear aim, overall policy and plan. Besides the above, lack of in depth knowledge of the Northeast states afflicted with insurgency, at the Centre, has lead to these problems being treated in a routine manner, or as merely one more issue. Mired in the routine, those dealing with it in the Ministry, cannot visualize feasible solutions to the complex problems of the region; well thought out measures or responses, are exceptions. With a reasonably large number of officers of the Army, Police, Para Military Forces (PMF), bureaucrats and knowledgeable academics who have grass root knowledge available, a selected expert group needs to be set up by the Centre to evolve policy(s), monitor and where required order execution of plans and policy(s), so as to achieve conflict resolution (select retired personnel, if any, can be appointed on a contractual basis). This group must be empowered to take decisions and direct measures to be taken; in no case should it be an adjunct of the Northeast desk of MHA. It should be under a separate minister for the Northeast or perhaps be an adjunct of the DONER Ministry. Though this group would be a part of the Central government, it should be located within the Northeast region – possibly at Guwahati/Dispur. In response to a possible argument that the National Security Advisory Board (NSAB) already exists for the purpose, it needs to be stated that the NSAB has a vast canvas to cover and its members may not have requisite knowledge of the Northeast region, besides, it is only an advisory body and has no executive powers, whereas the expert group being recommended, will be able to address issues specific to the Northeast and facilitate resolution of the problem.

Establishing "Unified Command"

The concept of 'unified command' has been accepted and set up to tackle insurgency in Assam and Manipur, after protracted efforts of the Army. The set up in Assam viz the 'Strategic Group is headed by the Chief Secretary i.e., functioning has been delegated to the state bureaucracy, in violation of the concept. Bereft of political involvement and direction, the organization suffers from bureaucratic hassles and inefficacy. The

'Operational Group' is headed by GOC 4 Corps.

In Manipur, the 'Combined Headquarters' has the Chief Minister as the Chairman, whereas the 'Strategic and Operational Group' is headed by the Chief Secretary; the principle of operational control by the lead agency to synergise operations, has been ignored thus negating the intended benefits of the concept. Besides, functionally the Chief Minister has delegated authority to the Chief Secretary with its concomitant fallouts. Until and unless the political leadership in the states gets actively involved and oversees the functioning, 'unified command' will continue to remain a mere concept and not achieve its evolved and stated aims.

Synergy between Various Intelligence Organisations

Though there is lack of synergy between the Army and various civil organizations in implementation aspects of the CI effort; this is the most glaring in the realm of intelligence. Lack of coordination and cooperation has come about, as each agency tends to pursue their own individual agenda by withholding information and indulging in 'one up man ship', at times even at the cost of larger gains. Though the unified command has an 'intelligence group' as part of its organization, the functioning is well below the desired standard. In the states where there is no unified command, intelligence sharing is virtually non existent. Another major weakness in the process of acquiring, collating, analyzing and disseminating intelligence is the assessment, which is more generic than specific, to ensure a safe fall back position for the authors of the intelligence. Total synergy amongst various intelligence agencies, be it civil or military, is the only way timely actionable intelligence can be provided to seriously impair operational capabilities of insurgent groups. Such a change can only come about if the political leadership allows these agencies to perform their primary tasks unhindered and instead provides positive directions for implementation of CI measures.

Informational Warfare

In this age of 'information explosion', the insurgent groups are techno savvy and use all available means to spread disinformation, propaganda, unleash psychological warfare to demoralize the state apparatus and create a feeling of despondency in the public. The Army has been making efforts to counter this propaganda and negate efforts of the insurgents, wherever they are conducting CI operations, regrettably these are not being supported by the state apparatus viz., the publicity department or the Press Information Offices; these organizations can fill in gaps of language, dialects, cultural and social aspects. Besides a synergized public information and counter propaganda initiative aimed at the common man is necessary in which the state machinery has an important role to play. Unfortunately, this segment of the state govt. apparatus is only utilized for collecting data for publishing in annual reports of achievements of the state government and may be some routine brochure/pamphlets and does not contribute to the CI effort. There is a requirement of setting up a Psychological Operations cell by the state government in concert with the local Army formation. A synergized effort in this regard will be a force multiplier for the CI effort and pay handsome dividends, since the common man does not have access to information except that put out by the vernacular media, which is a mouthpiece of the insurgent groups.

Development Projects

As highlighted earlier, only an insignificant amount of financial largesse given by the Centre is actually utilized for development purposes due to corruption and coercion; besides, there is no audit or accountability of the expenditure by the state government of funds provided by the Centre for some specific development projects. As no benefits of the development projects reach the masses, it leads to a feeling of neglect and further alienation amongst them, the states invariably misrepresent facts and blame the Centre for the lack of development. In some cases, the state administration may not be able to reach out to projects in far flung areas to ensure smooth execution and monitor progress. Politico-military cooperation can certainly provide an avenue to ensure successful completion of such projects as Army units/sub units are located almost everywhere and can certainly help in monitoring progress and providing factual feedback. This is only feasible if details of all such projects are shared with the Army; a step which the state authorities are loath to take. A joint approach in this regard will not only accelerate development per se with its concomitant spin offs, but assuage feelings of the masses to some extent also.

Institutionalized Mechanism to Obtain Inputs

Over a period of time, it has been observed that whenever required, the MHA summons the Chief Secretary and DG Police of the concerned state to obtain inputs on various current issues or an incident. However, no direct inputs are taken from the Army in the state, even if the incident involves them. It must be appreciated that the Army is as much involved in tackling the problem and in fact has primacy in conduct of operations. There is thus a necessity of evolving an institutionalized system of taking inputs from the Army as well. This would imply that if and when the Centre requires an update or inputs related to an ongoing issue or incident in an insurgency environment, the Army Officer at the helm of affairs in the state would also be part of team from that state. To those skeptical of this setting a wrong precedence, it merits mention that an arrangement already exists wherein IGAR(N), who is the Major General in-charge of all troops deployed in Nagaland, attends talks between the Govt. and the NSCN(IM) at Delhi, with the ADGMO(A), Army HQ also present; a similar system can thus be institutionalized wherever required. Besides giving definite impetus to politico military synergy, it will enable providing different inputs to the authorities at the Centre facilitating decision making.

Human Right (HR) Violations and Armed Forces Special Powers Act (AFSPA)

When under pressure due to security forces operations, the insurgent groups and their sympathizers invariably raise the bogey of HR violations and seek abrogation of the so called 'draconian' AFSPA. It merits mention that the AFSPA can only be imposed after the state government has promulgated the Disturbed Area Act (DAA) in whole or part of the state; this provision is reviewed every six months. In case the state or Central government does not promulgate DAA, AFSPA becomes inoperative (seven constituencies of Imphal town are outside the ambit of DAA and consequently the AFSPA since Aug 2004). Notwithstanding the above, it is imperative that there have to be legal provisions to provide protection to the troops conducting CI operations, be it in the form of AFSPA or Unlawful Activities (Prevention) Act 1967, suitably amended or any other legal provision. Without such provisions, troops will not be able to undertake any operations against insurgents but only react after being attacked i.e., in a defensive mode;

which is unacceptable operationally. Needles to state that those found guilty of HR violations must be dealt with in a transparent manner and utmost dispatch. Imposition of AFSPA is a political decision, however, politicians of the concerned state continue to find AFSPA a handy tool to beat the SF publicly; paradoxically, in private they state that it should not be revoked. With divergent views emerging from various organs of the state, insurgents exploit the AFSPA issue through the media; the security forces have to bear the flak, even in case of false allegations. No support is ever forthcoming to the Army from the state polity; instead politicians of the ruling party also are known to exploit even false incidents to score brownie points. If there is politico-military synergy on this issue, unwarranted conflagrations can be averted and false propaganda of the insurgents and their sympathizers negated.

Government Must Deal from Position of Strength

The manner in which events over the past decade have been handled by the Centre, be it the hijack of IC 814, the killing of BSF personnel by Bangladesh Rifles or our response to the Chinese aggressive diplomatic posturing or others, have only strengthened the perception of our adversaries that we are a 'soft' state. We did not even take a well considered stance on the issue of 'Nagalim' initially and have been vacillating thereafter, causing periodic turbulence in Manipur. The impression that we are a 'soft state' needs to be dispelled by the government by demonstrating its resolve, politically, diplomatically and militarily; the government must deal with the insurgents from a position of strength. To this end, we must have a clear stance on sanctuary and support to the insurgent groups by our neighbouring countries; we must retain the option of an armed response, besides resorting to coercive diplomacy. Setting up of an expert group, as suggested, will also be an indication of our resolve to deal with the situation in the Northeast and positive indicators of achieving politico-military synergy.

Illegal Immigration

Immigration of a large number of people illegally from Bangladesh into Assam, Tripura and West Bengal has resulted in a demographic inversion in the border districts of these states. A fallout of this has been sprouting of madrassas and illegal settlements in the vicinity of the border with their concomitant security implications. This potential security threat is regrettably being ignored for mere short term political gains. If not tackled with urgency, this is a handy tool for elements inimical to us to exploit for destabilization of the region and eventually for balkanization of the country. Besides revamping our immigration set up at the border, there is a need to examine the issue of work permits and enabling legal provisions need to be promulgated to deal with this menace. Politico – military synergy on this issue is perhaps inevitable, if we want to eradicate insurgency in the Northeast.

Countering the Foreign Element

The support to the insurgent groups including setting up of camps in Myanmar and Bangladesh is an incontrovertible fact of involvement of foreign elements. Despite intensified diplomatic efforts there has been no change in the ground situation. This is another arena where politico military synergy is vital. Governments in both these countries are being controlled by the Military. It would thus be prudent to allow our Army to increase interaction with the Army(s) of Bangladesh, Myanmar and PLA, in addition to the renewed diplomatic efforts. In case of persistent denials and in view of their aggressive behaviour with BSF in the past, we must exhibit our resolve by launching precision strike(s) on camps of IIGs in Bangladesh by our Special Forces.

There area number of other issues like revamping and rejuvenating the state bureaucracy and administration; strengthening, modernizing and training of the state police force(s) to tackle the insurgents, accountability of the state developmental institutions and others. These being outside the purview of the topic are not being discussed.

Conclusion

Mired in appalling under-development, with the rise of 'underground' economy comprising smuggling, extortion, fake currency, arms smuggling, narcotic and drug trafficking, the Northeast finds itself trapped in its economic backwardness. Insurgent groups have also shed the veil of ideology and are indulging in criminal activities. It is high time the local politicians also accept responsibility and develop a stake in the developmental process in their states, rather their own and resist from continuously pointing a finger at New Delhi, for all their 'ills'.

The importance of Northeast must not be ignored because the region is highly susceptible to external influences and its destabilization can lead to balkanization of the country. In order to achieve conflict resolution, political consensus across party lines is essential, so as to formulate an implementable and cogent strategy. As on today, at the executive end all organs of the respective states are engaged in fulfilling their own agenda, at the cost of the national aim. The main shortcomings are lack of cooperation, coordination and synergy amongst major organs of the state, dealing with the problem. The underlying issue is absence of faith in the Army by the political leadership and the bureaucracy, due to vested interests of the latter. Till the government does not share their perceptions related to security issues at the apex level with the hierarchy of the armed forces, signaling a change in their attitude towards them, the Army regrettably will not be able to deliver, not because of ability but because of denial of opportunity to do so. It is therefore, my earnest appeal to the powers that be, if 'Conflict Resolution' in the Northeast is the desired end state, let the Army be a party to arriving at a solution and not use it merely as in 'aid to civil authority' mode of yesteryears.

It must be realised that Northeast Region is India's near abroad - both in physical and mental aspects. India's policy seems to be to internalize the issue and to seek political accommodation for it rather than to have a strategic construct. As a result we have failed to realize the impact of peripheral states on politics, economics, demographics and security. Our Look East policy needs to start from our Northeast.

Economic Consequences of Conflicts in Northeast India

Gulshan Sachdeva

Introduction

Internal conflicts within the Northeast as well as political movements and armed rebellion against the Central government have shaped economic discourse in the region. Main reasons for these conflicts have been movements for independence and autonomy, discontent against outsiders, intra-tribal conflicts and discontent against Delhi. These factors have greatly influenced academic discourse, economic policy framework and subsequently economic performance in the region. The perception of insecurity created by conflicts have discouraged new investments and harmed further economic development. Traditionally, the economic literature on the region broadly discussed its unique economic institutions, 'economic backwardness' and failure of economic policies in the region.[1] The "mainstream" economic literature on the Northeast generally argued its economy in the context of "neglect" theory. It was frequently suggested that to end this neglect, massive developmental assistance from the Central government is required, which in due course would also end discontent, insurgency and terrorism in the region. Over the years, the region has undergone tremendous socio-political and economic changes. New research on the Northeast has also challenged some of these old perceptions. Still, policy makers deal with the region within the in the context of "tribal, backward, neglected and strategically important remote frontier". To achieve the objective of "balanced regional development", the Planning Commission deals with these States as "Special Category States". This paper argues that failure of economic strategy for the region is not because

---

[1] NirankarSrivastava, *Survey of Research in Economics on North East India 1970-1990*, (New Delhi: Regency Publications/ICSSR-NERC, 2000); *North East India: A Bibliography*, (New Delhi: Teen Murti Museum& Library,2002).

of any so-called economic neglect but because of wrong assumptions and inappropriate economic policy framework, which have created an unbalanced economy and destroyed the basic institutions of market economy. There is an urgent need to question usual myths surrounding the region, create market institutions and start working towards linking the region with the ASEAN neighbors. It is further argued that to take full advantage from its proximity to the ASEAN market, the region needs some fundamental changes in its land and labour policies in addition to improvements in infrastructure and security situation in some of the states. In the absence of these factors, the region will continue to depend on public investments for growth and development.

The Northeast

The Northeastern Region, traditionally known as the land of seven sisters, comprises the States of Arunachal Pradesh, Assam, Manipur, Meghalaya, Mizoram, Nagaland and Tripura, with about eight per cent of the country's geographical area and about four per cent of its population (45 million). Their combined contribution to the national economy is around two per cent. In 2002, Sikkim is also included in the grouping. Historically, successive legal and administrative decisions taken between 1874 and 1935 gave the areas of the North-East distinct identity. The British administration initially treated the hill areas as a "Non-Regulated Areas", declared them as "Backward Tract", "Excluded Areas" and "Partially Excluded Areas".

Statistics are available in plenty about the number of races, tribes and their sub-groups, ethnic groups, cultures, religions, languages and dialects spoken in this region but broadly speaking there are three distinct groups of people – the hill tribes, the plains tribes and the non-tribal population of the plains. The majority of those living in the plains are Hindus and Muslims while a substantial proportion of hill tribes in Meghalaya, Mizoram and Nagaland are Christians. Geographically, apart from Brahmaputra, Barak (Assam) and Imphal (Manipur) valleys and some flat lands in between the hills of Meghalaya and Tripura, the remaining two-third area of the region consists of hilly terrain. Most of this hilly portion is either owned, or controlled or managed, by tribes, clans or village communities. The most populous part is the Brahmaputra valley which constitutes about 22 per cent of the region.

The pace of development in the hill areas and plains differs considerably. The valleys are economically active areas, the Brahmaputra valley being the most active. Tribal population constitute only about one-fourth[2] of the population of North-East even though in four States — Mizoram, Meghalaya, Nagaland and Arunachal Pradesh — tribals are in majority. In Mizoram, which has one of the highest literacy levels (92 per cent) in the country, in 2001 they constituted as high as 95 per cent of the population. On the one hand, the region is diverse and heterogeneous. On the other hand, it is quite homogeneous; the social stratification found in other parts of the country is not present in the Northeast. The tribal societies in the hill areas are egalitarian. This results in better social indicators for most of the hilly States of the region.

On 26 January 1950, Northeast India consisted of the State of Assam and the Union Territories of Manipur and Tripura. However, to fulfill the political aspirations of the local people several new states, beginning with Nagaland in 1963 and ending with Mizoram in 1987, have been created. Further, there has been an increase in the number of districts in the tribal States of the Northeast. Mizoram with a population of only about eleven lakhs (2011) has eight districts. Administratively today the Northeast has eight states, 85 districts and 607 sub-districts. However, despite the creation of several new States and districts, the basic problem of integration and balanced economic development remains.

North East in Indian Planning Process

During the colonial period, the institutions and infrastructure in India were mainly developed to serve colonial interests[3]. In the initial years of planning after independence, regional economic development was still not really on agenda. The emphasis was on concentration of limited resources on those areas and regions which could give maximum returns to tackle the problems of food security and heavy dependence on imports for capital goods. Very little attempt was made at regional desegregation of national planning.

---

[2] According to 2001 census, tribal population of the Northeastern region (including Sikkim) constitute 26.93 per cent of the total population. for details see http://www.censusindia.net/t_00_005.html

[3] Krishna Bhardwaj, "Regional Differentiation in India: A note" *Economic and Political Weekly*, April 1982.

Emphasis on industrialization during the second plan led to some industrial regions. Although some problem regions like Damodar valley, refugee rehabilitation etc were identified, they were not part of any regional development strategy. Till that time, states of Northeast were not discussed as a "problem" region as per capita income of Assam was among the top few states.

In the third Five Year Plan, the concept of balanced regional development was discussed in detail. The policies through which the balanced regional development was supposed to be achieved were selection of industrial location (both for public and private sector), use of large projects as nuclei of regional growth, technological development, education and training and labour mobility. It was asserted that "from the decisions regarding location of projects in the public sector which has been reached so far, it is apparent that there will be a fair measure of dispersal and various regions will have significant share in industrial development"[4]. Despite these policy pronouncements, the third plan document also noted that "the level of development depends to a considerable extent on the availability of competent administrative and technical personnel and on the growth of a class of small and medium sized entrepreneurs... *Attention should be given to these aspects of development, for they point to handicaps which cannot be removed merely by providing resources to an under-developed region*" (emphasis added) [5]. This was an important observation, which was ignored in later plan documents. Overall, the thinking was that "development of regions and the national economy as a whole have to be viewed as parts of single process. Excessive emphases on the problems of particular regions and attempts to plan for their development without relating their needs to the requirements of the national economy have to be guarded against. In the final analysis, it is as integral part of the country that different regions can best hope to realize their full potential for growth."[6]

Fourth Plan outlined that "differences in development between states arise out of variations in activity in the three sectors—cooperative, private

---

[4] *Third Five Year Plan*, New Delhi: Planning Commission, p. 148.
[5] Ibid., p.151.
[6] Ibid., p.153.

and public". It was argued that in the cooperative and private sector, actions of the Central government could influence very little. In the public sector it was outlined that directions in which the Centre can help are: (1) allocation of Central assistance; (2) location of Central projects; and (3) adjustments in procedures and policies of national financial and other institutions. Apart from weightage given to backward states in the allocation of central assistance, programme for small farmers, marginal farmers, Drought Prone Areas, Dry Areas, Tribal Areas and industrially backward areas were also taken up. The Planning Commission also issued guidelines for the formulation of district plans. Despite these steps there was a sense of frustration in the Fifth Plan when it said that in the reduction of regional imbalances "the measure taken so far have not had any appreciable impact"[7]. It argued that "*there has been an unfortunate tendency to define the needed efforts merely in terms of financial magnitudes. Organisational and institutional aspects of the resource development problem of the backward regions have not been attended to.*" (emphasis added).[8]

Northeast as a region started figuring prominently in planning literature from the early 1970s, particularly after the reorganization of States in the region. The establishment of North Eastern Council (NEC) in 1972 was acceptance of the fact that this region needed special institutions and incentives for development. In the Sixth Five Year Plan, under the sub plan approach, greater emphasis was placed on Special Tribal Plan, Hill Area schemes and the programmes handled by the North Eastern Council [9]. Contrary to the Third Plan, where it was argued that the Central government cannot influence much the private sector initiatives in backward areas, under the Sixth Plan, Central policies were also designed "to provide incentives to private entrepreneurs through schemes of concessional finance, seed/margin money scheme, Central investment subsidies scheme, tax reliefs, specific interest subsidies for engineer entrepreneurs and so on"[10]. These policies were in addition to resource transfers and public sector programmes.

---

[7] *Fourth Five Year Plan*, New Delhi: Planning Commission, p.55.
[8] Ibid.
[9] *Sixth Five Year Plan*, New Delhi: Planning Commission, p.273.
[10] Ibid., p. 276.

One of the main objectives of the Seventh Plan was also the "adoption of effective promotional measures to raise the productivity and incomes of the poorer sections of the population, poorer regions and poorer States".[11] The Plan also emphasized the need for decentralisation of planning and development administration below the State level, particularly in the context of agricultural and rural development programmes. It urged the States to take steps towards four important aspects of a decentralised district level planning setup. These were (a) effecting functional decentralization (b) effecting financial decentralization;(c) the establishment of appropriate planning mechanism at the District level; and (d) establishment of appropriate budgeting and re-appropriation procedures.[12] In the eighth and ninth Five Year Plans, there were very little direct references of problems regions. In both these plans, Northeastern States were discussed broadly within the category of Special Area Development Plans like Hill Area Development Plan (HADP), NEC etc.[13] One of the major concerns of the midterm appraisal of the Ninth Plan as well as the Tenth Five Years Plan is that of widening regional disparities.

While emphasizing the importance of balanced development for all states, the Tenth Plan document included a state-wise break-up of the broad developmental targets, including targets for growth rates and social development. For the first time a separate volume State Plans was included. The document declared that, "the adoption of planning and a strategy of State-led industrialization were intended to lead to a more balanced growth in the country. It was expected that, over time, inter-state disparities would be minimized. Plans and policies were designed to provide more investments to the relatively backward areas. Nevertheless, socioeconomic variations across states continue to exist today."[14] It further said that some of regional imbalances have narrowed down, but most have grown over time.

---

[11] See Seventh Five Year Plan, Volume 1, http://www.planningcommission.nic.in/plans/ planrel/fiveyr/default.html

[12] See Seventh Five Year Plan, Volume II, http://www.planningcommission.nic.in/plans/ planrel/fiveyr/default.html

[13] See "Special Area Development Plans" in *Eighth Five Year Plan, Volume 2 http:// www.planningcommission.nic.in/plans/planrel/fiveyr/default.html*

[14] Tenth Five Year Plan, Volume III, (New Delhi: Planning Commission, Government of India), p.1.

To tackle the problem, it was argued that the emphasis would be on effectiveness, quality, and reforms and not so much on volumes of investment alone. According to the document, the "core element in the Planning Commission's strategy towards reducing regional disparities would be the targeting of less developed areas with provisions of funds for capital investments and innovative delivery mechanisms linked to institutional reforms."[15] . For the first time a special portion of the document deals with Northeastern States. According to the Tenth Five Year Plan "the trauma of partition, political evolution and insurgency combined with the geographical location, transport bottlenecks, natural calamities, etc., have hindered the progress of the North East, and the region has experienced relatively slower economic growth compared to the rest of the country. Most of the north eastern States joined the planned development process later than many other States."[16] The Plan documents outlined special measures initiated by the central government like the Special PM packages, NEC, non lapsable central pool of resources, Department of Development of the Northeast etc.

The Eleventh Five Year Plan argued that it was the collective endeavour of the Central and State governments to form appropriate polices for the region. The plan document emphasized connectivity (road, rail, air, inland waterways, and telecommunications) as the key area for the development of Northeast. In addition, it was recognized that economic activities would be generated through interaction with neighbouring countries.[17] The draft twelfth plan document asserts that the region has "witnessed encouraging growth during last two Plan periods" This it is argued is "primarily due to the investments in the major projects by the Centre and the developmental programmes taken up by the States".[18] Critical areas identified by the plan where intervention is still needed are roads, railways, airways, inland water transport, power, agriculture, water management, skill development and encouragement to private investment.

---

[15] Ibid.,p.124.

[16] ibid, p 91.

[17] See *Eleventh Five Year Plan 2007-2011,* Volume 1 (New Delhi: Planning Commission, 2008) pp. 151-164.

[18] *Draft Twelfth Five Year Plan (2012-2017),* Volume 1, (New Delhi: Planning Commission, 2012), p. 336.

Understanding Economic Policy Framework for the Northeast

Above analysis shows that the policies of regional development provide some scattered information about the Northeast. Although, many of the recent government documents do provide some special mentions of the Northeast, they are not shown as part of any coherent strategy. They also do not clearly mention any linkages or diversions from the earlier policies.

It seems that due to special constitutional arrangements, historical background as well as geographical location,[19] the Central government has been trying to integrate the Northeast region with the national economy through certain policy framework. It has accepted the right of tribals to retain their way of life and identity and has sought to integrate them through democratic means into the federal frame of the Constitution of India. The policy framework for the region so far is guided by a combination of political economy and culture. The main focus of the *political economy approach* is on the relations between the state and the economy. Therefore, in this approach, the role of the bureaucratic state arrangements is strongly emphasized. The *cultural approach*, however, focuses on the socially constructed character of economic organization where the economic system is a product of the social order.

---

[19] Some of these special historical and geographical aspects of the region as well as background of special constitutional arrangements are nicely summarized by L P Singh ," Problem (The North-east: A Symposium on the Problem of a Neglected People & Region), *Seminar*, No. 336, 1990.

Figure 1

```
┌─────────────────────────────────────────────────┐
│   Economic Policy Framework for the Northeast     │
└─────────────────────────────────────────────────┘
```

The Political Economy Approach
(main emphasis on the role
of state and its bureaucratic
arrangements in economic
development)

The Social Approach
(Focus is on socially
constructedcharacter of
economic organistaion)

outcome

```
┌─────────────────────────────────────────────────┐
│   Instead of creating an efficiency oriented      │
│   economic process, the framework results         │
│   in a politically led distribution oriented process │
└─────────────────────────────────────────────────┘
```

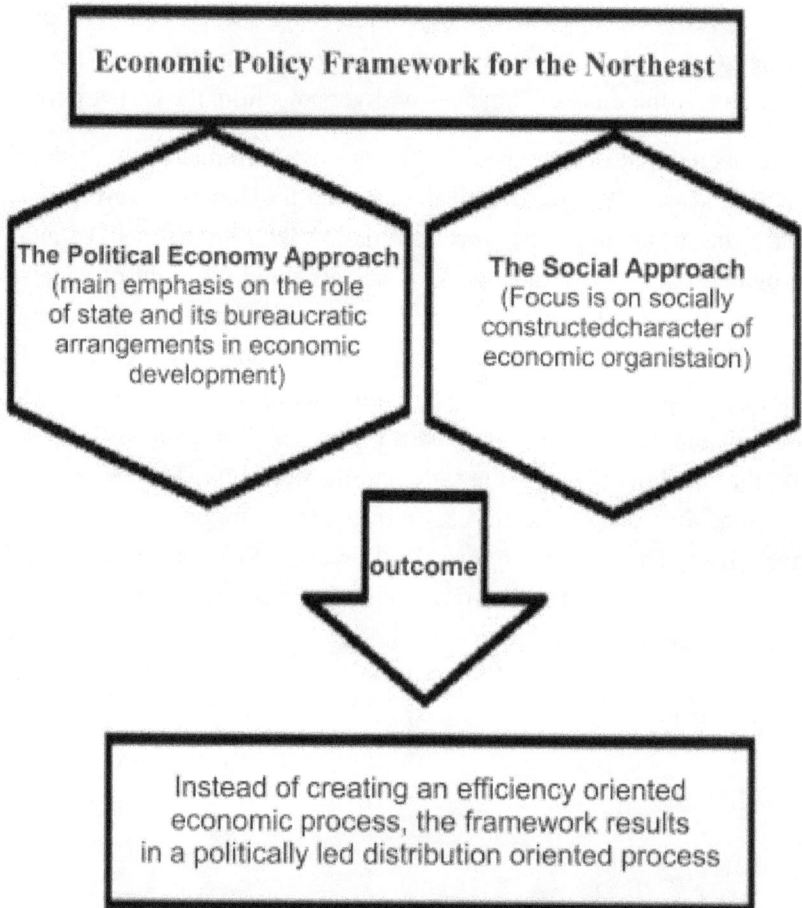

As a result of this combined approach, the importance of the bureaucratic arrangements in the process of economic development has been unduly exaggerated. Besides, wherever possible, an attempt has been made by policy makers to work through the unique social and cultural institutions existing in the region instead of imposing new institutions.[20] This special approach has been adjusted with the central governments' policies of a regional planning development model. The major assumption of regional planning is that it would permit the transfer of surplus generated in one region to another. This mechanism was expected to increase aggregate national efficiency through optimum resource allocation.

Under the influence of this policy, various schemes for the development of infrastructure and economy of the North-East region have been formulated. The schemes include the formation of the North-Eastern Council, Hill Area Development Projects and sub-plans, Tribal Area sub-plan, and Tribal Development Agency Projects to name only a few. In addition, these seven states have been declared as Special Category States; they get Central Assistance on the basis of 90 per cent grant and 10 per cent loan. Some public sector units have also been set up in the region. The policies of industrial licensing, concessional finance and investment subsidy, growth centres, as well as freight equalization of some major industrial inputs have also been used towards economic development. Under the announcement made by the then Indian Prime Minister Deve Gowda in October 1996, all developmental Ministries and departments of the Central government have been directed to earmark at least 10 per cent of their gross budgetary support (GBS) for the Northeast. In case any Central government ministry failed to achieve this target, the unutilized 10 per cent portion is pooled in the Non-Lapsable Central Pool of Resources (NLCPR) which will be re

---

[20] While writing the forward to the second edition of *A Philosophy for Nefa* by V Elwin, V (1959), Pt. Jawaharlal Nehru wrote that "avenues of development (for tribal areas) should be pursued within the broad framework of the following five fundamental principles:

(1) People should develop along the lines of their own genius and we shoulda v o i d imposing anything on them. We should try to encourage in every way their own traditional art and culture.

(2) Tribal rights in land and forests should be respected

(3) We should try to train and build up a team of their own people to do the work of administration and development. Some technical personnel from outside will, no doubt, be needed, especially in the beginning. But we should avoid introducing too many outsiders into tribal territory.

(4) We should not over-administer these areas or overwhelm them with a multiplicity of schemes. We should rather work through, and not in rivalry to, their own social and cultural institutions.

(5) We should judge results, not by statistics or the amount of money spent, but the quality of human character that is evolved.

utilized to finance developmental projects in the Northeast. Creation of a separate department of Development of North Eastern Region (DONER) was another new initiative by the government. This department has now been converted into a ministry viz. Ministry of Development of North Eastern Region.

Further, to protect tribal interests, policies of less interference with the cultural traditions and customs of the tribal people are being followed and additional political and administrative framework has been provided for the region.Under the sixth schedule of the Constitution, the concepts of Autonomous District Councils, regional councils and territorial areas have also been applied.[21] The councils are responsible for looking after the social, economic and minor criminal and civil matters of the tribal people. More specifically these councils are empowered to make laws with respect to: a) Land; b) Forest; c) Water course; d) Shifting cultivation; e) Establishment of village and town and its administration; f) Appointment of, or succession to chiefs or headmen; g) Inheritance of property; e) Marriage and divorce and matters relating to any other social customs.

Restrictions have been imposed on the rights of citizens of other states as well as non tribals from the same state to acquire landed property in some parts of the Northeast. The regulation of Inner Line Permit prohibits entry of outsiders into Arunachal Pradesh, Mizoram and Nagaland without a permit, and debars a non-native to acquire any interest in land or the produce of land. Tribal belts and blocks have been constituted in the plains areas to prevent tribal land alienation.

Public Investment Dependent Economic Outcomes

The development strategy followed by the Centre and state governments has created a totally unbalanced economy in the Northeast. There are differences among all states of the region with respect to their resource endowments, levels of industrialisation as well as infrastructural facilities. On the whole, all these economies are underdeveloped agrarian societies

---

[21.] See R N Prasad, " Sixth Schedule and Working of the District Councils in the North-Eastern States" Dialogue Quarterly, Vol 6, No.4, 2004;, Arvind K Sharma " District Councils in the North-East" in T N Chaturvedi, ed., *Fifty Years of Indian Administration: Retrospect and Prospect.* New Delhi: Indian Institute of Public Administration, 1998.

with very weak industrial sectors and inflated service sectors. The share of agriculture although declined, still much higher than the national average. The industrial sector has mainly developed around tea, oil, timber (TOT) in Assam and mining, saw mills and plywood factories in other parts of the region. The tea plantation industry employs a large labour force, in Assam alone it employs more than 500,000 workers. State sponsored industrialisation — whether sugar mills, jute mills, paper mills or food processing has not been successful. Small scale industries have also not been viable and there is large scale industrial sickness in this sector. Despite changes, the economy of the region remains primarily agricultural. The full potential of this sector has not been exploited. Primitive farm practices of slash and burn (jhum), shifting cultivation in the many of the hills and mainly single crop traditional farming in the plains continue. As a result, the region is not even able to produce adequate food grain to feed its population. The states of the region import food items worth about Rs 2,000 to Rs 2,500 crores annually from other parts of the country. Since neither agriculture nor industry has taken off, the pressure for employment is on the service sector (means government service). As a result, this sector has expanded disproportionately. Because of low economic activity, the states of the region have resource deficit. Of these limited resources a large portion is spent mainly to maintain the service sector.

The regional average growth rates in the 1980's were slightly lower than the national economy. During this period except Assam, all other economies in the region grew at higher growth rates than the national economy. Growth was close to national economy even in the case of Assam. In the post-liberalisation phase during the nineties, while the national economy was growing fast after initial contraction, overall Northeastern economy slowed down. As a result, the gap between national growth rates and regional growth rates further widened. Assam, the largest economy of the region was in a very critical state, both in agriculture and industry. In the decade of eighties, the average rate of growth Assam was more than 4 per cent. In the nineties, growth in Assam was much lower. Except Arunachal, the hill economies have not shown much difference in growth rates in the last twenty years or so. Tripura economy in fact has grown fast in the 1990's. As a result of these trends it could be concluded that gap between the northeast and the national economy widened in the nineties. The improved agricultural production and productivity in some pockets of North-East, however, indicated that there was a large untapped potential in agriculture.

As economic difficulties led to many social and political tensions, the Central government took many initiatives, particularly from the mid-nineties. After seeing difficult economic conditions, State governments from the region also initiated many measures to attract private investment. As a result, economic performance in the last few years has improved significantly, particularly in Assam. This seems to have resulted from large inflow of resources from the Central government and agricultural growth in Assam and some other parts in the region. Even earlier, the Northeastern region was never a "neglected" region as far as devolution of resources from the Central government to region is concerned. These resources have increased substantially in the last one decade.

At present, more than 50 Central Ministries/ Departments earmark 10 per cent of their gross budgetary support for the Northeast. Between 1998-99 and 2006-07, these Central Ministries/Departments spent about Rs 44909 crore out of total earmarked fund of Rs 53294 crore on Northeast. According to the Planning Commission the spending figures for these Ministries on the Northeast during the Eleventh Plan (2007-12) is likely to be about Rs 75,000 crore (out of their total earmarked funds of about 87,000 crore for the region). Overall, the total Plan expenditure by the Centre and the states of Northeast, including NEC, was about Rs123,756 crore during the four years of the Eleventh Plan (March 2011) through various windows of funding (including Central assistance provided to the States under their plan, NLCPR, and NEC and Centrally sponsored schemes etc. Out of which Rs 57,000 crore were provided through State Plans, Rs 59,000 crore through different Central Ministries and Rs 7,500 crore through NEC and DONER. This is likely to go upto Rs 150,000 crore by the end of the plan.[22]

These planned investments have helped the region to come out of low growth trap of the nineties. This has become possible because of reemergence of growth in the biggest economy of the region, i.e Assam. The economy of Tripura has been showing strong growth performance

---

[22] For details see Chapter "Regional Equality" in the *Draft Twelfth Five Year Plan*, Volume 1 (New Delhi: Planning Commission, 2012).

consistently in the last twenty years, perhaps because of better targeted programs. Growth in other smaller hilly economies is heavily dependent on resources from the central government for their economic performance. Economic situation is certainly better than the nineties (because of improvement in agriculture in Assam). Still, the fundamentals of the Northeastern economy remain the same. It is still difficult to visualize strong growth in hilly economies based on private investment and improved chances of transit trade.

Average Annual Growth Rates in the Northeast under Different Five Year Plans, 1992-2017

	Eighth (1992-97)	Ninth (1997-2002)	Tenth (2002-07)	Eleventh (2007-2011)	Twelfth (2012-17) (Target)
Arunachal Pradesh	5.1	4.4	6.5	9.4	8.3
Assam	2.8	2.1	5.3	6.9	7.1
Manipur	4.6	6.4	5.7	6.5	6.6
Meghalaya	3.8	6.2	6.4	8.1	8.0
Mizoram	-	-	5.7	11.0	8.6
Nagaland	8.9	5.7	5.9	6.2	7.2
Sikkim	5.3	7.8	7.8	22.8	8.4
Tripura	6.6	6.4	6.4	8.7	7.9
All India	7.5	5.3	7.8	7.9	8.2

Source: Draft Twelfth Five Year Plan, 2012-17, Volume 1 (New Delhi: Planning Commission, 2012), pp. 316,332

State-wise and Sector-wise Targeted Growth Rates for the Northeast during the Twelfth Five Year Plan (2012-2017)

	Agriculture	Industry	Services	Total
Arunachal Pradesh	5.5	9.0	10.0	8.3
Assam	4.8	4.7	9.0	7.1
Manipur	5.3	5.0	8.5	6.6
Meghalaya	3.1	8.8	9.0	8.0
Mizoram	6.9	9.9	9.0	8.6
Nagaland	4.5	9.0	8.0	7.2
Sikkim	4.0	8.0	10.0	8.4
Tripura	5.0	8.0	9.0	7.9
All India	4.0	8.0	9.1	8.2

Source: Draft Twelfth Five Year Plan, 2012-17, Volume 1, (New Delhi: Planning Commission, 2012), p. 316.

Need to Demystify the Northeast

"Complex, mysterious, unique" the region is continue to be referred to in these terms in academic, media and policy circles. Indeed, the region's history, geography, ethnic composition and culture have given it a distinctive character. And selective academic research on disparate subjects like tribal customs, community ownership, gender equations etc, has generated interest. The Central government deals with these states as "Special category States". Although, over the years, the region has undergone tremendous changes but certain stereotypes have remained. For most people in policy circles, media and academia, it still remains a tribal, neglected, backward, insurgency prone remote frontier. The time has come to question some myths surrounding the region. This will help create a meaningful ground for future policy making.

Any discussion regarding the region starts with its tribal nature. It is almost unanimously accepted as a tribal region. Surprisingly, facts on the ground are totally different. According to 2001 census, only about one-fourth of the population of the region is tribal. It is always emphasized that in the four States — Mizoram, Meghalaya, Nagaland and Arunachal Pradesh — tribals are in majority. But tribal majority in these states does not make the whole region tribal. Moreover today in Northeast, tribals are not "head hunters"; on the contrary, a large number of them are educated and have adopted western dress and modes of living. It would be misleading to equate them with marginalized tribals in other parts of the country. Since independence, Indian policy makers have been very sensitive to the tribal nature of the region. Some of these policies we have discussed in the earlier sections. Earlier many scholars critically looked at this protective policy as they found that it had failed to stop alienation of tribal land.[23] Prof B K Roy Burman asserted that as a result of this policy, a process of "state or bureaucracy sponsored neo-feudalization" was taking place in the region.[24] In recent years, this policy framework has been under attack from different reasons. The policy of protective discrimination for Scheduled Tribes in the region raises serious questions of justice, and equality for the non-tribal population.[25] As Sanjib Baruah argues that this kind of policy "effectively compromises the constitutional right to free movement of Indian citizens".[26] Moreover, rigid barriers – which aim at restricting outside penetration –are contrary to the processes of contemporary globalization.[27] In these circumstances, it would be more productive and useful if we start treating Northeastern economic problems in a normal way rather than in a "special tribal way". First, the region is not a "tribal region" and secondly, "special solutions" have created more problems than solving it.

---

[23] B N Bordoloi, 'Land Alienation among Tribes of North-East India: Problems and Policies" *IASSI Quarterly*, Vol 12, Nos. 3 & 4, 1994, pp. 17-48; M N Karna, "The Agrarian Scene", *Seminar*, No 366, February 1990, pp 30-38.

[24] B K Roy Burman, " Land and Forest Rights" *Seminar,* No. 336, pp.25-29.

[25] SanjibBaruah, "Protective Discrimination and Crisis of Citizenship in North-East India*" Economic and Political Weekly*, April 26, 2003.

[26] SanjibBaruah, *Durable Disorder: Understanding the Politics of Northeast India*, (New Delhi: Oxford University Press, 2005), p. 51.

[27] For details see GulshanSachdeva, *Economy of the North East, Policy, Present Conditions and Future Possibilities,* New Delhi: Konark Publishers, 2000.

Secondly the myth about "neglect" the region needs to be seriously researched. There is obviously some neglect of the Northeast in Delhi politics and national media. There could also be some knowledge deficit. But most vocal writings and speeches regarding "neglect theory" often cite economic figures to show the neglect. National institutions like the Planning Commission are of little help. In fact, some of its main publications have created more confusion. For example, the *National Human Development Report 2001*[28]used poverty ratios of Assam for Sikkim, Arunachal Pradesh, Meghalaya, Mizoram, Manipur, Nagaland and Tripura. As a result, poverty ratio of states like Nagaland, Mizoram etc was shown very high, although other indicators like infant mortality ratios and consumption expenditure surveys of the National Sample Survey Organisation gives a different story altogether. While using these kinds of figures, many scholars created theories of neglect and underdevelopment. Fortunately, in recent years, the discourse is changing. Both the North Eastern Human Development Report and Draft Twelfth Five Year Plan documents reveal relatively balanced picture concerning the Northeast.

There could be any other kind of neglect but the facts about devolution and transfers of resources from the Centre reveal entirely different story. Between 1990-91 and 2002-03, the region received about Rs 1,08,504 crore. A portion of that money is also given back to the Central government as repayment on loans and interest payments. Still, the cumulative net devolution from the Centre to the Northeast for the period between 1990-91 and 2002-03 is about Rs 92,000 crores. Only grant portion to the region during these 13 years was about Rs 65,000 crores.[29] So the lack of development could not be because of shortage of funds. Economist and Congress leader Jairam Ramesh has also argued that this kind of public expenditure has become very much part of the problem of the Northeast.[30] In fact, a significant portion of development funding actually ends up in the hands of underground groups.

Thirdly the importance of high literacy levels in the Northeast should not be overemphasized. Although the region has done well due in education

---

[28] See table notes at pp. 164-166 and Technical Appendix page 133 in the *National Human Development Report 2001*, New Delhi: Planning Commission, 2002.

[29] Authors calculations based on Reserve Bank of India as well as CMIE publications.

[30] Jairam Ramesh, "Northeast India in New Asia", *Seminar*, No. 550, June,2005.

because of many socio-historical factors, yet some serious problems remain. A recent *Human Development Report of North Eastern States* (2011) has concluded that "in general, the Northeastern states are perceived to be doing fairly well in human development as compared to states in other regions of the country".[31]

Even high literacy rates in the Northeast are accompanied by low educational levels due to high dropout and low standards. Active student politics and the culture of *bandhs* in the region have played havoc with the education system. There are enough teachers in the region but many of them are not trained. According to the *Human Development Report of North Eastern States 2011*, at middle and upper primary level only 17 per cent teachers in Nagaland, 27 percent in Arunachal, 32 per cent in Manipur and 36 per cent in Meghalaya were trained. The corresponding figure for the national level was about 87 per cent.

Another factor which has to be understood is that major parts of the region face labour scarcity. This is perhaps one of the main reasons for the failure of various labour intensive government schemes like animal husbandry, Jawahar Rozgar Yozana etc. Despite all the talk of outside invasion, labour (both skilled and even unskilled in hilly states) is a big problem with the possible exception of Brahmaputra valley and Tripura. Already outside labour (mainly from Bangladesh, Myanmar, Nepal and other parts of India) is a crucial factor in both agricultural as well as non-agricultural activities. With any increase in economic activities, the problem of labour shortage is expected to be aggravated. Unless the Inner Line restricted areas are opened for outside labour, economic development is going to suffer. Or worse it would be an open invitation to illegal Bangladeshi immigrants.

Issues Concerning Look-East Policy

Another standard argument in the past has been the disadvantageous geographical situation of the Northeast. This has been argued in writings as one of the main stumbling block for its economic development. This isolated, landlocked region shares less than 1 per cent of its borders with the rest of

---

[31] *Human Development Report of North Eastern States* (New Delhi: DONER, 2011), p.6.

the country, and the rest with Bhutan, Bangladesh, Myanmar and China. For the most part this international border was artificially created. The result has been the elimination of the region's trade, commerce and other linkages which existed in the pre-partition days. Using the region's two per cent perimeter as a major linkage point with the rest of India and at the same time checking the inflow of goods and people from across the remaining rest of 98-99 per cent has been a gigantic task.

In the last one decade, there have been serious discussions on converting this locational disadvantage into a boon because of an increasingly integrated world economy.[32] This is particularly so when all the states of the region are on international borders. In addition, these states are very close to the dynamic Southeast and East Asian economies. Most policy makers in the region are excited and optimistic about the idea of linking their economies with dynamic Asia. There were even suggestions that if for security reasons the Government of India is reluctant to open up the natural trade routes, the Northeast states should ask the Central government to compensate them for the loss of trade.[33]

These arguments gained momentum at a time when India's "Look East" policy was being implemented.[34] Right from the sixties to the eighties, India and East Asia retained their mutual suspicions. However, the nineties were to mark a significant change in their relations. India had met with limited success in improving its relations with East Asian nations bilaterally during the eighties. The early nineties brought far reaching changes at the global scene. With the collapse of the Soviet Union and the end of the Cold War ideological division of the world ended. After the Soviet collapse, India was also looking for diversification in its foreign trade links. The rapid economic growth of these countries had also made solid impact on the prevailing inward economic thinking in Indian academia and policy elite.

---

[32] See "Gateway to the East: A Symposium on Northeast India and the Look East Policy" Seminar, No. 550, June 2005.

[33] *Report of (Jayanta Madhab) Committee on Industry,* Volume 1, Dispur; Government of Assam, *1996,* p.6.

[34] For details see CharanWadva and GulshanSachdeva" Indian Perspectives on East Asia" in CharanWadhva and Yuen Pau Woo (eds) *Asian Regionalism: Canadian & Indian Perspectives,* (New Delhi: APH Publishing Corp, 2005).

Many think tanks in the West had started predicting next century as the Asian century.[35] Against this background, India started working for its "Look East" policy. The crux of this initiative was not just pushing Indian exports to East Asia or attracting investment from the region. The idea was to start an entirely new relationship with the East Asian region in all areas encompassing political, economic, strategic and cultural areas.

These developments were going to have a significant impact on the Northeast. The reason being that there was not only a failure of the economic policy framework in the region but also a weakness of country's foreign policy which had ignored Southeast Asia for a long time. As a result, the Northeast region was not only cut off from its natural economic partners but also encircled by unfriendly countries. Now with this broad policy changes in India's foreign policy, many scholars and policy makers have started talking about advantages of linking Northeast with the ASEAN markets.

So far the major border trade activity of the region with Bangladesh and Myanmar is through 'unauthorised trade'. The state authorities are fully aware of these activities which function smoothly through unofficial channels. China is an important player in the border trade even though its trading activities are mainly through Myanmar. The major policy issue, therefore, would be to synchronize these realities into Indian trade policies.

There is however, a danger that the hype of linking Northeast with Southeast Asia becoming another myth if we do not prepare the region step by step. While keeping the long term goal in mind, at this point the emphasis should be on creating conditions, both at the policy level and at the ground level, on converting the unauthorized trade into authorized trade. This is not a simple task. The genuine trader will have many practical problems. The unauthorized trade works on the basis of a strong network which involves traders, police, forest departments and, of course, many underground groups and each has its own share in the pie. Apart from infrastructural problems at Moreh, the large number of check posts on National High Ways 39 and 53 would a create problem in switching over from illegal to legal trade. In most cases, the State governments turn a blind eye to the border trade in

---

[35] SanjayaBaru, "The Problem", *Seminar*, March 2000.

illegal items because it creates a lot of economic activity in the region. Since these commodities are not declared legal officially, there is corruption at every turn. The important point is that first of all the region should start producing globally competitive products. For that many of the issues concerning land tenure policies, inner line regulations, Restricted Area Permits, infrastructure, security issues have to be tackled. Otherwise, the region would be a transit point of goods which may create further discontent.

Conclusion

Many scholars have argued that one of the major reasons for conflicts in the Northeast has been marginalization and underdevelopment of its economy. The prevailing security situation in some parts of the region has created disincentive for new investments and harmed further economic development. So conflicts in the Northeast are firstly result of developmental model applied in the region and secondly an obstacle to further economic development. The weakness of economic strategy for the region is not because of any so-called economic neglect but because of wrong assumptions and inappropriate socio-economic policy framework, which have created an unbalanced economy and destroyed the basic institutions of market economy. To fulfill political aspirations of local people, many new States as well as special arrangements through Schedule 7 of the constitution have been created. Many of these policies might have served some political purpose but have created huge economic problems. Some of the small States have become economically dependent on the Central government resulting in bad governance, patronage and corruption. To protect tribal interests, a complex land tenure system is in operation in most parts of the region which has not allowed commercial agriculture in about two-third of the Northeast. Besides, land has become a serious source of conflict between increasingly declining tribal populations and non-tribal citizens in the Northeast. The Inner Line Regulations and Restricted Area permit system might have hindered movement of investment, tourism and genuine skilled manpower; it has not been able to stop large scale illegal migration across the border. The discontent against the Centre and outsiders has provided enough ideological motives for many insurgent groups to continue to operate in the Northeast. These insurgencies have been sustained with money collected through extortions and cuts from liberal government funds. Difficult security situation has necessitated continued presence of armed forces.

But the presence of these forces and isolated incidents of abuse and human rights violations have angered and further distanced citizens and civil society from state institutions. The prevailing law and order situation in many parts of the region, attitude towards outsiders, scarcity of land and skilled labour and insufficient infrastructure created disincentives for private investment and which could have led to domestic production and integration of the economy to the dynamic Asian neighborhood.

Overall there is need to demystify the region, create basis institutions of the market economy and start working towards linking it with dynamic Asian economies. Due to large public investments, growth situation in the region has improved in the region, particularly in Assam. Still, in a liberalized environment, we should concentrate more on economic factors and less on political and cultural factors. The economic factors include labour cost, comparative advantages, technology, efficiency and returns on investment. In a new environment, the inefficient economic processes (jhum) and barriers to market entry (inner line regulations, restricted area permits, trading licensees, existing land tenure policies in hilly areas etc) will clearly make an economic difference. Due to strategic factors and complex political economy situation in India, the Central government will continue to support smaller Northeastern economies.The actual action concerning any fundamental change regarding land policies, inner line regulations, law and order and above all changes in attitude towards investors (read outsiders) will begin only at the state level. Once the capacities to deal with these issues are created at the State/regional level, it is quite natural that Northeast will be able to take advantage from its close proximity to the Asian markets. With prospects of legitimate economic activities improving, some of the conflicts may also fade away.

Contributors

Mr M.K. Narayanan is the Governor of West Bengal. He is an alumnus of the Loyala College, Madras, and holds a Master's Degree in Economics from the University of Madras. He joined the Indian Police Service in 1955. Most of his service career was spent in the Intelligence Bureau under the Government of India. He was Director of the Intelligence Bureau from 1987 to 1992 and also served as the Chairman of the Joint Intelligence Committee of the Government of India. Mr Narayanan was awarded the prestigious national award Padma Shri in 1992. He is a founding member of CSA and was its Vice President till May 2004. He was appointed as the Security Advisor to the Prime Minister of India in May, 2004 and January, 2005 as the National Security Advisor to the Prime Minister of India.

Ms Ancy Joseph is research assistant at the Centre for Security Analysis, Chennai. She has written articles on the conflict and the current affairs of Myanmar as well as on internal conflicts in South Asia. As a Research Assistant at CSA, she assists the Executive Director in carrying out the Center's programmes and projects. She holds a Master of Philosophy Degree in Public Administration and Masters Degree in International Studies and Public Administration from the University of Madras.

Brig. K. Srinivasan (Retd) is a graduate of Defence Services Staff College and College of Defence Management, during his active army career of 35 years, participated in 1965 and 1971 wars and in counter insurgency operations in Jammu & Kashmir and has held several important command, instructional and planning assignments. At Centre for Security Analysis (CSA), he guides and supervises the work of research fellows. His area of work includes, conflict resolution & peace building, terrorism, disaster management and role of civil society in conflict situations. He has been an active member of the working group on Disaster Management and Water Security convened by Strategic Studies Network set up by National Defense Univeristy, Washington, DC.

Falguni Rajkumar is a scion of the erstwhile ruling family of Manipur. He is the first direct recruit IAS officer from the Meitei community of

Manipur. He worked in the Ministry of Petroleum and Natural Gas, the Ministry of Defence as Joint Secretaries for five years each and in the rank of Secretary to Government of India as Secretary of the North Eastern Council, Shillong in the Ministry of DoNER from where he retired in 2009. After retirement he worked as Special Advisor of UNIDO dealing with the North East region of India. Shri Rajkumar is at present the Chairman of the Board of Governors of the Rajiv Gandhi Indian Institute of Management, Shillong. He has authored a book "The Rainbow People: Reinventing Northeast India."

Monalisa Changkija is a journalist, poet, writer and a social activist from Nagaland. She has been associated with several newspapers and magazines within and outside Nagaland. She is proprietor, publisher and editor of Nagaland Page, a daily English newspaper. She is noted for her hard-hitting editorials, especially on social issues. Her first hand reports on the First Merapani War (1985) waged between the Police Forces of Assam and Nagaland for the first time, brought to the fore the role of women in conflict situations. She was awarded 2009 Chameli Devi Jain Award for Outstanding Women Media person. Her poems and short stories are part of the curriculum in schools and university in the state. She has presented numerous papers at national and international fora on Naga issues, Women's role in conflict situation, Human Rights and media. She is also associated with numerous non-governmental organisations and think-tanks in the Northeast region.

Samir K Purkayastha is a freelance writer and journalist based in Kolkata. He has 19 years of experience in working for reputed newspapers in the Northeast, in various capacities like Bureau Chief to Associate Editor. Presently he is working on his maiden book, Peril of Peace. Samir has extensively covered conflict situations, peace processes, migration and trans-border issues confronting Northeast, for national as well as regional papers like The Telegraph, The Asian Age, The Sentinel, The Seven Sisters Post, The Nagaland Page and The Nagaland Observer, among others.

Jayanta Kumar Ray is Research Fellow, Maulana Abul Kalam Azad Institute of Asian Studies, Kolkata. He has vast teaching experience spanning over forty years. He had authored, edited and co-edited numerous books. His articles have been published in reputed national and international journals.

Maj Gen Arun Roye (Retd) is former General Officer Commanding, Bengal Area and presently the Executive Director and Secretary, the Research Centre for Eastern and North Eastern Regional Studies (CENERS-K) Kolkata. He held the appointment of the ADG Assam Rifles under the MHA in our North Eastern Region. He holds post graduate degrees in Defence Studies from Madras University and College of Defence Management. He has trained the Bhutanese Army, did the Command and General Staff Course in erstwhile USSR and held the assignment of Military Advisor in Indian Embassy, Washington DC, USA.

Prem Das Rai, Member of Parliament from Sikkim. He joined active politics in 1994. Mr. Rai has contributed immensely to the building of the NGO sector in Sikkim. He continues to interact with civil society groups. He has a deep understanding of the geopolitics of the Northeastern region and instrumental in setting up the Sikkim Studies Program in the Centre for NE studies at the Jamia Milia Islamia, New Delhi. He is also intensely involved in the India Chapter of Global Legislators Organisation for Balanced Environment (GLOBE) and is working toward Climate Change Legislation in India.

Major General Sheru Thapliyal (Retd) is a graduate of Defence Services Staff College Course, Higher Command Course and National Defence College Course. He has served in many Planning and Operations Directorates at Army Headquarters. He is an elected member of the governing council of United Services Institute and a member of Institute of Defence Studies and Analysis, Institute of Peace and Conflict Studies, Institute of Chinese Studies, Observer Research Foundation and Delhi Policy Group.

Prof Gulshan Sachdeva is a Professor at the School of International Studies, Jawaharlal Nehru University (JNU), New Delhi. His areas of interests include European studies, regional cooperation and issues concerning Afghanistan and Northeast India, energy security, development aid and India's relations with the EU, Russia & Central Asia. He is a regular contributor to national print and broadcast media on both economic and security issues. He has authored the book *Economy of the Northeast (2000)*, and various monographs, project reports and more than 80 research papers in scholarly journals and edited books. He holds a Ph.D. in Economic Science from the Hungarian Academy of Sciences, Budapest.

CSA Publications

Books

Conflict Resolution and Peace Building

1. Conflict Resolution and Peace Building in Sri Lanka

2. Federalism and Conflict Resolution in Sri Lanka

3. Peace Process in Sri Lanka: Challenges & Opportunities

4. Conflict over Fisheries in the Palk Bay Region

5. Conflict in Sri Lanka: The Road Ahead

6. Peace and Conflict Resolution: Emerging Ideas

7. From Winning the War to Winning Peace: Post War Rebuilding of the Society in Sri Lanka

8. Internal Conflicts in Myanmar: Transnational Consequences

9 Internal Conflicts in Nepal: Transnational Consequences

10. The Naxal Threat: Causes, State Responses and Consequences

11. Conflict in Sri Lanka: Internal and External Consequences

12. Conflicts in North-East: Internal and External Effects

13. Conflict in Jammu and Kashmir: Impact on Polity, Society and Economy

14. Post Conflict Sri Lanka- Rebuilding of the Society

15. Internal Conflicts: Military Perspectives

16. Internal Conflicts: A Four State Analysis

17. Nepal as a Federal State: Lessons from Indian Experience

Security Studies

18. US and the Rising Powers: India and China

19. Maritime Security in the Indian Ocean Region: Critical Issues in Debate

20. Public Perceptions of Security in India: Results of a National Survey

21. Essential Components of National Security

22. Economic Growth and National Security

23. Security Dimensions of India and Southeast Asia

24. India & ASEAN: Non-Traditional Security Threats

25. Emerging Challenges to Energy Security in the Asia Pacific

26. Security Dimensions of Peninsular India

27. Socio-Economic Security of Peninsular India

Civil Society and Governance

28. Civil Society and Governance in Modern India

29. Civil Society in Conflict Situations

30. Civil Society and Human Security: South & Southeast Asian Experiences

Bulletins

1. Nuclear Terrorism and Counter Proliferation: Issues and Concerns; After the Afghanistan and Iraq Wars: Perspectives from the US; Indo-Pak Relation: Limited War to Limited Peace?

2. Unconventional Weapons and Threats of Accidents and Terrorism; The Stability- Instability Paradox: South Asia and the Nuclear Future; Post 9/11: New Research Agenda?; The US and India: Divergent and Convergent Interests

3. Conflict Prevention and Peace Building

4. Indo-Japan Relations; Independent Police Complaints Commission; Brief on the Seminar on Security Dimensions of Peninsular India

5. Proceedings of the Seminar on Proliferation Security Initiative

6. Proceedings of the Seminar on Women and Legal Security

7. Political Islam: Image and Reality; UK and India on the World Stage

8. Proceedings of the Seminar on Women and Comprehensive Security

9. Global Nuclear Weapon Prospects; India-Pakistan Peace Process Dividends

10. Security Perspectives from Pakistan; Indo-US Relations: Changing Perceptions

11. Sri Lankan Peace Process: Current Status; Sri Lanka Today: Policy Challenges and Dilemmas

12. Religion, Civil Society & Governance

13. Politics of the Nuclear Deal and the US-India Relations

14. India –US Relations; Japan India Partnership in the New Asian Strategic Dynamism

15. Environmental Security; National and International Security in the Context of Globalization and Economic Prosperity; India, East and Southeast Asia: Security Dimensions

16. India-EU Relations

17. India-Japan Strategic Partnership; India-UK Economic and Business Partnership.

18. Right to Information

19. A Sustainable Future: India and Britain Working Together; India and Africa: Issues of Globalization and Development

20. New Initiatives in Nuclear Disarmament; Preventing Nuclear Proliferation and Nuclear Terrorism; Nuclear Fuel Supply Assurances

21. The Economic Cost of the War in Sri Lanka; Peace Process in Sri Lanka; The Sri Lankan Diaspora: The Way Forward

22. Nuclear Deterrence and Disarmament

23. Naxalism: Threat to Internal Security; Ethno-Political Situation in India's Northeast.

24. Japan and Asian Security; India as a Superpower.

25. India's Water Relations with her Neighbours

www.ingramcontent.com/pod-product-compliance
Lightning Source LLC
Chambersburg PA
CBHW030852270326
41928CB00008B/1330